NOTES TO OFFICIAL USERS

Air Ministry Orders and Vol. II leaflets as issued from time to time may affect the subject matter of this publication. It should be understood that amendment lists are not always issued to bring the publication into line with the orders or leaflets and it is for holders of this book to arrange the necessary link-up.

Where an order or leaflet contradicts any portion of this publication, an amendment list will generally be issued, but when this is not done, the order or leaflet must be taken as the over-riding authority.

Where amendment action has taken place, the number of the amendment list concerned will be found at the top of each page **affected**, and amendments of technical importance will be indicated by a vertical line on the left-hand side of the text against the matter amended or added Vertical lines relating to previous amendments to a page are not repeated. If complete revision of any division of the book (e.g. a Chapter) is made this will be indicated in the title page for that division and the vertical lines will not be employed.

June, 1941   AIR PUBLICATION 1721B
                                       Pilot's Notes

LIST OF SECTIONS

(A detailed Contents List appears at
the beginning of each Section)

Section 1.   Controls and equipment for pilot

Section 2.   Handling and flying notes for pilot

R.T.P/869. 1050. 6/41

AIR PUBLICATION 1721 B
Pilots Notes

BRISTOL BEAUFIGHTER PILOT'S FLIGHT OPERATING INSTRUCTIONS

PILOT'S NOTES

BEAUFIGHTER II AEROPLANE

TWO MERLIN XX ENGINES

Prepared by direction of the
Minister of Aircraft Production

Promulgated by order of the Air Council.

AIR MINISTRY

AIR PUBLICATION

Volume I

Pilot's Notes

AMENDMENT CERTIFICATE

Incorporation of an amendment list in this publication should be certified by inserting the amendment list number, initialling in the appropriate column and inserting the date of incorporation.

Holders of the Pilot's Notes will receive only those amendment lists applicable to the Preliminary Matter, and Sections 1 and 2.

Amendt. List No.	7C	9D	14E	15F	19G	20H				
Prelimy. matter										
Leading Partics.										
Introducn.										
Section 1			✓	✓	✓	✓				
Section 2	✓	✓	✓	✓	✓	✓				
Section 3										
Section 4										
Section 5										
Section 6										
Section 7										
Section 8										
Section 9										
Section 10										
Section 11										
					June 1943	Aug 2/43				
Date of incorpn.	Incorporated					KH.				

Amendt. List No.	25										
Prelimy. matter											
Leading Partics.											
Introducn.											
Section 1	✓										
Section 2	✓										
Section 3											
Section 4											
Section 5											
Section 6											
Section 7											
Section 8											
Section 9											
Section 10											
Section 11											
Date of incorpn.	26/8/44 FR										

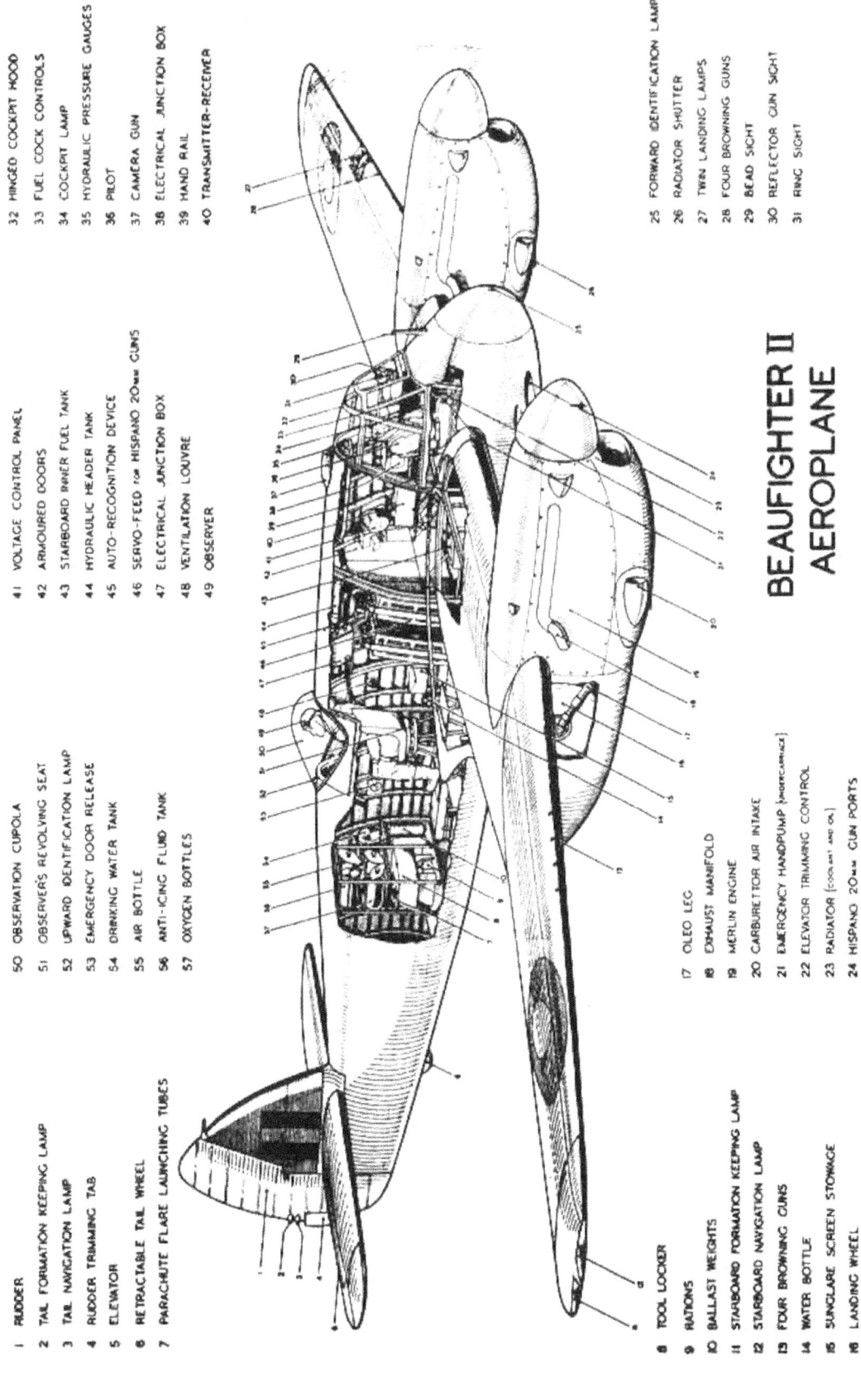

BEAUFIGHTER II AEROPLANE

1. RUDDER
2. TAIL FORMATION KEEPING LAMP
3. TAIL NAVIGATION LAMP
4. RUDDER TRIMMING TAB
5. ELEVATOR
6. RETRACTABLE TAIL WHEEL
7. PARACHUTE FLARE LAUNCHING TUBES
8. TOOL LOCKER
9. RATIONS
10. BALLAST WEIGHTS
11. STARBOARD FORMATION KEEPING LAMP
12. STARBOARD NAVIGATION LAMP
13. FOUR BROWNING GUNS
14. WATER BOTTLE
15. SUNGLARE SCREEN STOWAGE
16. LANDING WHEEL
17. OLEO LEG
18. EXHAUST MANIFOLD
19. MERLIN ENGINE
20. CARBURETTOR AIR INTAKE
21. EMERGENCY HANDPUMP (UNDERCARRIAGE)
22. ELEVATOR TRIMMING CONTROL
23. RADIATOR (COOLANT AND OIL)
24. HISPANO 20mm GUN PORTS
25. FORWARD IDENTIFICATION LAMP
26. RADIATOR SHUTTER
27. TWIN LANDING LAMPS
28. FOUR BROWNING GUNS
29. BEAD SIGHT
30. REFLECTOR GUN SIGHT
31. RING SIGHT
32. HINGED COCKPIT HOOD
33. FUEL COCK CONTROLS
34. COCKPIT LAMP
35. HYDRAULIC PRESSURE GAUGES
36. PILOT
37. CAMERA GUN
38. ELECTRICAL JUNCTION BOX
39. HAND RAIL
40. TRANSMITTER-RECEIVER
41. VOLTAGE CONTROL PANEL
42. ARMOURED DOORS
43. STARBOARD INNER FUEL TANK
44. HYDRAULIC HEADER TANK
45. AUTO-RECOGNITION DEVICE
46. SERVO-FEED FOR HISPANO 20mm GUNS
47. ELECTRICAL JUNCTION BOX
48. VENTILATION LOUVRE
49. OBSERVER
50. OBSERVATION CUPOLA
51. OBSERVER'S REVOLVING SEAT
52. UPWARD IDENTIFICATION LAMP
53. EMERGENCY DOOR RELEASE
54. DRINKING WATER TANK
55. AIR BOTTLE
56. ANTI-ICING FLUID TANK
57. OXYGEN BOTTLES

Revised by A.L.14/E   A.P.1721B Vol.I & P.N.,Sect.1.

LIST OF CONTENTS

	Para.
INTRODUCTORY	1
FUEL SYSTEM	
Fuel tanks	2
Fuel gauges & cocks	3
HYDRAULIC SERVICES	
General	4
Hydraulic power lever	5
AEROPLANE CONTROLS	
Primary controls.	6
Primary controls locking gear	7
Flying instruments	8
Elevator trimming tabs control	9
Rudder trimming tab control..	10
Aileron trimming tab control.	11
Undercarriage control..	12
Undercarriage control safety lock.. ...	13
Undercarriage radius rod locking pins ...	14
Undercarriage position indicators and warning horn ...	15
Flaps control and position indicator ...	16
Hand pump..	17
Wheel brakes ... ,..	18
Dive brakes	19
ENGINE CONTROLS	
Throttle and mixture controls	20
Propeller speed controls	21
Ignition controls	22
Two-speed supercharger controls	23
Carburettor air-intake controls	24
Automatic boost control cut-out	25
Carburettor cut-out controls.	26
Fuel cocks	27
Starting booster coil switches	28
Priming pumps	29
Starter controls.	30
Worth oil dilution	31
SEATS DOORS AND WINDOWS	
Pilot's seat	32
Entrance...	33
Direct vision panels...	34
COCKPIT EQUIPMENT	
Heating controls.	35
Height and airspeed computor stowage and map case...	36
Sunblind...	37
Water bottles	38
Flying ration boxes	39
Rear vision mirror	40

Revised by A.L.14/E

	Para.
OPERATIONAL EQUIPMENT	
Gun sights	41
Gun firing controls	42
Flares	43
Camera	44
Oxygen equipment	45
RADIO & INTERCOMMUNICATION EQUIPMENT	
Intercommunication signalling	46
Radio equipment (early aeroplanes)	47
Radio equipment (later aeroplanes)	48
LIGHTS & SIGNALLING EQUIPMENT	
Navigation	49
Identification lights	50
Formation keeping lights	51
Auto-recognition control	52
Landing lamps control	53
Signal pistol	54
DE-ICING EQUIPMENT	
Propeller de-icing	55
Windscreen de-icing	56
Pressure head heating	57
EMERGENCY EXITS AND EQUIPMENT	
Emergency exits	58
Dinghy release	59
Fuel jettison control	60
Fire extinguishers	61
Axe	62
First-aid outfit	63
Emergency rations	64
Emergency signalling	65
R.3003 or R.3078 destruction	66

LIST OF ILLUSTRATIONS

	Fig.
General view of cockpit	1
Pilot's Intrument panel	2
Port side of cockpit	3
Starboard side of cockpit	4
Emergency exits and equipment	5
Flying Control locking gear	6
Fuel system diagram	7

Revised by A.L.14/E.　　　A.P. 1721B Vol.I & P.N., Sect.1.

BEAUFIGHTER II
SECTION 1

PILOT'S CONTROLS & EQUIPMENT.

INTRODUCTORY

1. This Section gives the location and, where necessary, explains the function and operation of the controls and equipment in the pilot's cockpit, and also of equipment that is located elsewhere but with which the pilot should be acqainted. The layout of the various items and instruments is illustrated and referenced in figs. 1 to 4. The number after an item is the reference number in figs. 1 to 4.

FUEL SYSTEM

2. Fuel tanks.-

   (i) There are two main tanks, inner and outer, on each side as shown in fig. 7.

   (ii) Later aeroplanes also have additional long range tanks - shown by dotted lines - which form in effect enlarged outer main tanks These long range tanks displace the wing guns which are not fitted on aeroplanes so equipped.

   NOTE: As an interim measure pending the fitting of long range tanks as described in sub-para. (ii) some aeroplanes have a 50 gallon tank fitted amidships between the pilot and observer. Fuel is transferred from this tank by means of a handpump worked by the observer. The delivery pipe leads into the main balance pipe to starboard of the balance cock which should be on during transfer. This tank obstructs the passage between pilot and observer and a wire and pulley message conveyor is fitted for intercommunication purposes.

3. Fuel gauges and cocks.-

   (i) Contents gauges (59) & (83) are fitted for all tanks. On later aeroplanes with long range tanks the gauges for these are on the rear of the front spar on the starboard side. A master switch (78) controls all these gauges.

Revised by A.L.14/E.

    (ii) Fuel pressure gauges (40) & (41) (on later aeroplanes replaced by low pressure warning lights) are on the instrument panel. They are controlled by the contents gauges master switch (on later aeroplanes by the undercarriage indicator switch).

    (iii) <u>Fuel cocks</u>.- See para.27

HYDRAULIC SERVICES

4.   <u>General</u>.- The hydraulic system operates the undercarriage and tail wheel retracting gear, and the flaps. Normally, fluid under pressure is supplied to the actuating jacks by two pumps, one on each engine. A hand pump, mainly for servicing, but also for emergency operation of the alighting gear and flaps is also provided in the pilot's cockpit. The controls for operating the hydraulic system are situated on the port side at the base of the pilot's instrument panel. Two gauges mounted on the port handrail show the delivery pressure of the port and starboard pumps.

5.   <u>Hydaulic power lever</u>.- (1) This operates a valve which directs fluid either for the operation of the alighting gear and flaps or through the by-pass. For alighting gear and flaps operation, the lever should be down in the ON position, but, unless these services are being used, it should be in the OFF position, when the aeroplane is flying. As otherwise the engine driven pumps may overheat and sustain damage. When on the ground, however, the lever should be left in the ON position.

AEROPLANE CONTROLS

6.   <u>Primary controls</u>.- These are conventional in design and operation and the pendulum type rudder pedals are adjustable for reach by a handle under the instrument panel.

7.   <u>Primary controls locking gear</u>.- Locking gear for the primary flying controls is stowed in the roof slightly to port above the handrail. The method of locking the controls is as follows:- See Fig.6.

    (i) Hold the control column in the central position.

    (ii) Insert the eyebolt on the gear through the hollow bolt at the bottom of the column and secure with the pin.

Revised by A.L.14/E.   A.P.1721B Vol.I & P.N., Sect.1.

    (iii) Attach the aft end of the gear by the quick-release pin to the top of the bracing tube on the port side of the pilot's seat.

    (iv) Fix the clip on the aileron handwheel.

    (v) Fix the clips on the rudder pedals.

8.   <u>Flying instruments</u>.- The usual instruments are mounted on the pilot's instrument panel. There is a vacuum pump driven by each engine with a change-over cock (51) to enable either pump to be used. On early aeroplanes only there is a vacuum gauge (49) beside the cock.

9.   <u>Elevator trimming tabs control</u>.- The elevator trimming tabs are controlled by a handwheel (72) at the top of a column mounted on the starboard side. The handwheel is mounted fore-and-aft and operates in the natural sense. An indicator (89) showing the position of the tabs is mounted on the starboard side of the column supporting the handwheel.

10.   <u>Rudder trimming tab control</u>.- The rudder trimming tab is controlled by a handle (73) mounted in a horizontal position on the starboard side close to the base of the pilot's instrument panel. The control operates in the natural sense. An indicator showing the position of the tab is incorporated on the handle.

11.   <u>Aileron trimming tab control</u>.- The trimming tab on the starboard aileron is controlled by a handle (86) mounted on the starboard side in line with the back of the pilot's seat. The control operates in the natural sense. An indicator showing the position of the tab is incorporated in the handle. The tab on the port aileron can be adjusted only on the ground.

12.   <u>Undercarriage control</u>.- The undercarriage and tail wheel control lever (10), which has a black knob, controls the raising and lowering of the undercarriage units and of the tail wheel unit. The movement of the lever is in the same sense as the movement of the units, i.e., up to raise the units and down to lower them.

Revised by A.L.14/E.

13. **Undercarriage control safety lock.-** In order to prevent inadvertent retraction of the alighting gear when the aeroplane is on the ground, the control lever is automatically locked in the DOWN position by the safety lock. The lock consists of a spring-loaded pin connected by a cable to the ram of the inboard shock absorber leg of the starboard undercarriage unit. When the weight of the aeroplane is on the undercarriage and the shock absorber frame is compressed, the cable is slack and the pin is forced by the spring into a position where it obstructs the movement of the control lever to the UP position; when the aeroplane is in flight and the weight is removed from the undercarriage, the shock absorber frame moves downwards and the pin is withdrawn. If necessary, the lock can be overridden by depressing the thumb catch mounted on the lever.

14. **Undercarriage radius rod locking pins.-** A further positive means of preventing inadvertent retraction of the undercarriage when the aeroplane is on the ground is provided by locking pins fitted, directly by hand from the ground, into the knuckle joints of the inboard radius rod of each undercarriage unit. A red flag is attached to each pin and the pins must be removed before flight.

15. **Undercarriage position indicators and warning horn.-** Three electrical position indicators (13) one on each side for the corresponding undercarriage unit and one in the middle for the tail wheel unit, are mounted on the port side of the instrument panel above the hydraulic control levers. When the three units are locked in the retracted position, the indicators show the word UP on a red background, and, when the units are locked in the lowered position, they show the word DOWN on a green background. When the units are not locked in either the up or down positions, or the indicators are switched off, black and white dazzle lines are shown at the centre of the indicators. There is also in the nose of the fuselage, an electrical warning horn that sounds if the engine throttle levers are closed beyond about the one-third open position and remains in operation with the throttle levers in this position until the undercarriage units are locked down. The switch (48) for the undercarriage and tail wheel position indicators is fitted beside the main magneto switches.

Revised by A.L.14/E.   A.P.1721B Vol.I & P.N.,Sect.1.

The indicator switch knob is fitted with an extension bar which, in the off position of the switch, obstructs the movement of the magneto switches from the off to the on position. When the indicators are switched on by moving the switch knob sideways to the left, the bar is withdrawn from the magneto switches.

16. *Flaps control and position indicator*.- The flap control lever (11), which has a black knob, controls the lowering and raising of the split-trailing-edge flaps. Its movement is in the same direction as the movement of the flaps, i.e. down to lower the flaps and up to raise them. When setting flaps to an intermediate position return the lever to NEUTRAL as soon as the desired setting is reached.

17. *Hand pump*.- This pump draws fluid from a reserve in the header tank and is operated by a handle (90) to starboard of the pilot's seat; it is used:-

   (i) For emergency lowering of the flaps and undercarriage through separate pipe lines. To use this system the hydraulic power lever (1) must be set off and the emergency selector (2) on. The emergency selector must never be on unless the hydraulic power lever is off and on some aeroplanes an interlock prevents this. This system lowers the flaps as well as the undercarriage when their control levers are set to either the up or down positions; with the flap control lever at neutral the undercarriage only will come down and to lower the flaps subsequently the flap lever must be set to down. On later aeroplanes an interlock returns the flap lever to neutral when the emergency selector is set on; with this arrangement the undercarriage only will come down unless the flap lever is first set to down.

   (ii) For ground operation of the normal system as an alternative to the engine driven pumps when these are not running. For this purpose the emergency selector must be off and the power lever on. The hand pump should not be so used in flight except in accordance with (iii) below.

   (iii) For operating the undercarriage and flaps through the normal system as in (ii) in the event of failure of the emergency system. To do this the emergency selector must be off, the hydraulic power lever on, and the flaps and undercarriage lever set up or down as required. See section 2 para 23.

Revised by A.L.14/E.

18. **Wheel brakes**.- The pneumatic brakes are operated by a lever (7) on the handwheel. For parking, a spring loaded catch retains the lever in the on position. To engage, depress lever, then set catch and release lever. To disengage, depress lever when catch springs clear.

   NOTE.- On certain aeroplanes there is a lock fitted to the tail wheel to hold it central while taking off and landing. The control for this is a push-pull handle to the right of the pilot's seat. To free the wheel pull up. To lock, press the small knob on handle then push down.

19. **Dive brakes**.- Some aeroplanes are fitted with dive brakes consisting of flaps fitted above and below each wing. They are retained in the closed position by the air flow, assisted by suction generated by a venturi tube. The flaps have a bellows device and there is a valve in the venturi tube which, when closed, diverts air pressure to the bellows so forcing the flaps into the open position. The valve is controlled by a lever mounted on a box former by the engine controls. This lever is pushed forward to apply the brakes and back to close them. It must be operated smartly and must not be set to an intermediate position.

ENGINE CONTROLS

20. **Throttle and mixture controls**.- Two throttle control levers (61) and a single mixture control lever (62) are mounted on a quadrant on the engine control panel at the left hand side of the pilot's seat. The throttle lever slots are marked SHUT at the rear end and TAKE-OFF at the front. There are no gates. The mixture lever is marked RICH at the rear end and WEAK at the front. The controls incorporate a trip mechanism between the throttle levers and the mixture lever. The mixture lever if in the WEAK position is automatically returned to RICH when the throttle is closed, the trip mechanism coming into operation at approximately $15°$ from the SHUT position.

21. Propeller speed controls.- The levers (60), outboard of the throttle and mixture lever, control the Rotol 35° constant speed propellers. The forward position of the lever gives maximum r.p.m. and the extreme aft position positive coarse pitch. On later aeroplanes there is a gate which obstructs movement of the lever to the positive coarse pitch position, but when required the lever can be moved beyond this gate to the positive-coarse-pitch position by applying side pressure.

22. Ignition controls.- The main magneto switches (46) are on the instrument panel.

23. Two-speed supercharger controls.- Two-speed supercharger controls (69) are mounted in a quadrant aft of the throttle and mixture controls on the engine control panel. There are two positions only to which the lever should be moved, forward to fully supercharged marked S and rearward to medium supercharged marked M.

24. Carburettor air-intake controls.- The air-intake shutter levers (56) are situated on the outboard side of the two-speed supercharger controls and control the supply of either cold or hot air to the carburettors. The lever for the port engine air intake has a red knob and that for the starboard has a green. The levers are set forward for cold air and back for hot air.

25. Automatic boost control cut-out.- This is for emergency use only. The control is wired at the engine end; to operate the lever (70) is pushed smartly forward, this breaks the wire and operates the cut-out.

26. Carburettor cut-out controls.- The carburettor cut-out controls (52) are in a control box with a spring-loaded hinged cover fitted to the top of the front spar on the port side. The controls have a red knob for the port engine and a green for the starboard. To stop engines pull knobs out.

27. Fuel cocks.- The contorls for the three cocks of the fuel system are mounted under the sill sube on the port side. The handwheels (53) and (54) control the tank cocks and the lever (55) controls the suction balance cock. The small handwheel controls the starboard tanks cock and is coloured green and the large handwheel controls

Revised by A.L.14/E.

the port tanks cock and is coloured red. Each handwheel, has three positions clearly marked on the rim, TANKS OFF, OUTER TANKS ON, INNER TANKS ON, and ball catches register with holes when the selected cock position is uppermost. The handwheels are rotated in a clockwise direction from the TANKS OFF position to open the cocks. On later aeorplanes there is a knob on each wheel. These are at the top in "TANKS OFF" position. The knob of the lever that operates the suction balance cock is coloured black. The lever should be moved down to open the cock.

28. Starting booster coil switches.- These (35) & (36) are mounted on instrument panel.

29. Priming pumps.- These are also mounted on the engine nacelles and are accessible when the undercarriage is extended.

30. Starter controls.- The push buttons (31) are on the instrument panel.

31. Worth oil dilution.- This system is fitted to later aeorplanes. The operating switches are on the engine nacelles.

SEATS DOORS AND WINDOWS

32. Pilot's seat.- The pilot's seat is constructed to take a seat type parachute, and is adjustable for height by means of a lever (65) on the left-hand side; the lock for securing the seat at the desired height can be released by turning the twist grip at the end of the lever. A seat-collapsing lever is also fixed to the right-hand side of the seat pan for use by the pilot when making an emergency exit. To collapse the seat the lever should be up and pressure applied from the shoulders to the top of the seat back. This action breaks the junction of the seat back and pan, and straightens them out for the next exit operation. To return the seat to the normal position, pressure should be applied to the bottom of the seat back. Sutton safety harness is fitted to the pilot's seat and the shoulder straps are anchored to a special fitting on the seat back in order that the pilot may lean forward without unfastening his harness. The extension is obtained by operating the lever on the right-hand side of the seat back. When the pilot leans back agains, the catch automatically snaps home into position.

Revised by A.L.14/E.   A.P.1721B Vol.I & P.N., Sect.1.

33.   Entrance.-

(a) For pilot.- Entrance to the fuselage is through a hatch in the underside of the fuselage between the centre-plane spars. To open the hatch a handle just forward of the hatch is pulled. This releases the bottom catch and the hatch is swung open and pushed home into the top catch. Entrance can then be made by the ladder attached to the hatch. Two hand grips and two handrails are provided. The hadn grips are situated, one on the starboard keel member and one on the port bracing tube for the front spar. The hand-rails are situated in the roof of the fuselage. To shut the hatch, release the top catch either from the inside by the handle situated on the starboard side just above the floor or from the outside by the handle just forward of the hatch. Swing the hatch shut and push home into the bottom catch. The hatch is opened from inside by pulling a lanyard attached to a lever on the port side of the fuselage just aft of the front spar. This releases the bottom catch. The hatch is then pulled up by the lanyard attached to it and pushed into the top catch.

(b) For observer.- A similar hatch for the observer is situated in the underside of the rear fuselage just aft of the observer's seat, and is operated on the same principle but there is no lanyard.

34.   Direct vision panels.- On each side of the pilot's windscreen are direct-vision windows (4) for use if the windscreen is obscured. The windows open inwards on hinges at the outboard sides, and are retained in the closed position by draw bolts which are locked by knurled knobs. Before opening a window, the knurled knob must be slackened right back. On later aeroplanes there is a simpler type of catch.

COCKPIT EQUIPMENT

35.   Heating system controls.- The port and starboard heating systems are controlled from the pilot's cockpit and the observer's station respectively. The port system handle (66) controls the cockpit heating and is situated just outboard of the pilot's seat to port. Hot air is admitted to the cockpit when the handle is in the forward position.

Revised by A.L.14/E.

The starboard system supplies hot air to the 20 m.m. gun compartments as well as to the observer's station

36. Height and airspeed computor stowage and map case.- A map case with stowage for a height and airspeed computor is fitted on the side of the engine control panel below the hydraulic controls.

37. Sunblind.- A sunblind is provided above the pilot's head; it is fitted with a tab and hook to enable it to be pulled forward and secured in an eye at the forward end of the wire rails on which it slides.

38. Water bottles.- Two water bottles are stowed in the rear fuselage at the base of the observer's seat.

39. Flying rationboxes.- One is stowed in the rear fuselage at the base of the equipment crate, a second on the starboard wall opposite the crate.

40. Rear vision mirror.- On Coastal Command aeroplanes there is a rear-vision mirror on the front edge of the cockpit roof.

OPERATIONAL EQUIPMENT

41. Gun sights.- A reflector gun sight, with a dimmer switch insorporated is mounted on a bracket attached to the starboard side of the windscreen sill. By means of a slot in the bracket and a knurled locking screw the sight can be clamped in its operational position or stowed clear of the pilot's vision. Three spare lamps for the gun sight are stowed in a holder on the starboard side.

42. Gun firing controls.- There is a firing button on the control handwheel. This fires the wing guns. A trigger (not shown) operates the cannon guns. On early aeroplanes the button (6) fires wing guns, cannon guns, and the camera simultaneously.

43. Flares.- The two forced landing flares, when carried, are released pneumatically. The control (74) consists of two shielded push-buttons. The forward button releases the port, the aft button the starboard flare.

Revised by A.L. 14/E. A.P.1721B Vol.I & P.N., Sect.1.

44. **Camera.-** On early aeroplanes the camera is fired by the gun-firing button (6) on later aeroplanes there is a separate button (not shown) also on the wheel. A master switch (87) and fusebox are on the starboard side, and the footage indicator with its socket, and socket stowage adjacents, is mounted on the wedge plate (84).

45. **Oxygen equipment.-** Two (on later aeroplanes three) cylinders supply oxygen to a standard regulator (58) with (on some early aeroplanes) a bayonet socket (80) on the starboard side. On later aeroplanes an economiser replaces the socket. Similar equipment is installed at the observer's station.

RADIO AND INTERCOMMUNICATION EQUIPMENT

46. **Intercommunication signalling.-** On the starboard side of the instrument panel is a push-button unit (34) which operates a buzzer and a white light on the observer's instrument panel in the rear fuselage Also on the unit is a lamp operated by the observer from a similar unit.

47. **Radio equipment (early aeroplanes).-** These are equipped with a combined transmitter-receiver either type T.R.9D or T.R.1133A. The microphone telephone socket is fitted on the starboard side adjacent to the aileron trimming tab control. A remote controller is fitted on the port side aft of the hydraulic controls and a master contactor is mounted on the centre plane floor under the transmitter-receiver. The master contactor switch (57) is mounted below the mechanical controller. Mounted above the master contactor is a switch controlling the heating element. The heating element should always be switched off when the pilot leaves the aeroplane.

48. **Radio equipment (later aeroplane).-** The following radio equipment is fitted:-

   (1) Fighter Command

   T.R.1133A - Twin sets, port and starboard are fitted, Controllers, NORMAL and SPECIAL switch, and remote contactor indicating disc are in pilot's cockpit port side.

Revised by A.L.14/E

A.1271 - Used in conjunction with the starboard (on some aeroplanes either) T.R.1133A for beam approach. Switch in pilot's cockpit, port side.

A.1219 - At observer's station below hood. Used in conjunction with the port T.R.1133A. Intercommunication switch in pilot's cockpit, port side.

T.3065) - In rear fuselage at observer's station
R.3066)   on starboard side. Visual indicator for observer. Alternator cut-out switch in pilot's cockpit, port side.

R.3003 or) - At observer's station under his
R.3078   )   control.

(ii) Costal Command

T.R.9 - Remote controls, and NORMAL and SPECIAL switch, are in pilot's cockpit, port side.

T.1154) - At observer's station under his control.
R.1155)

A.1134 - At observer's station. Used in conjunction with T.1154 and R.1155.

R.3003)
  or   - As in Fighter Command aeroplanes.
R.3078)

D.F.Loop - At observer's station. Additional visual indicator in pilot's cockpit, port side.

R.1124A) - The controls in the pilot's cockpit are as
R.1125A)   follows:- Remote controller, starboard side; mixing switch, port side; visual indicator on instrument panel, port side.

  NOTE: This standard beam approach is also fitted in some early aeroplanes (both Commands).

LIGHT AND SIGNALLING EQUIPMENT

49   Navigation:- The navigation lamps are controlled by the front switch of the 3-unit switchbox (77) above the compass on the starboard sill tube.

Revised by A.L.14/E   A.P.1721B Vol.I & P.N., Sect.1.

50.   Identification lights.- The signalling switching
            (76) on the starboard side of the cockpit provides
            for the independent or simultaneous use of the
            upward and downward identification lamps through
            the morsing key or, alternatively, a steady
            illumination from the lamps. The desired downward
            lamp or lamps (red, green or clear), should be
            selected on the 3-unit switchbox (75) forward of
            the signalling switchbox.

51.   Formation keeping lights.- The signalling switchbox
            (79) on the starboard side of the cockpit provides
            the morsing or steady illumination from the forma-
            tion-keeping lamps; only the DOWNWARD switch is
            wired.

52.   Automatic-recognition control.- The control for
            the auto-recognition device is situated on the
            starboard side high up behind the pilot's seat.
            To operate the device the handle is pulled, this
            fires one cartridge. The handle is then re-
            turned to the in position and the device is
            again ready for use. The device is situated aft
            of the rear spar and contains five cartridges.
            On later aeroplanes the device is mounted so as
            to fire upwards and the operating handle mounted
            on the starboard side, in the box former, in line
            with the pilot's shoulder.

53.   Landing lamps control.- The landing lamps control
            lever (67) is situated on the inboard side of the
            two-speed supercharger controls and controls the
            dipping of both landing lamps in the leading edge
            of the port wing. To depress the lamp beam, the
            lever should be pushed forward. Gates are
            provided on the lever quadrant for retaining the
            lever in the up position or in the dipped position.
            Each lamp has a completely independent electrical
            circuit and is controlled by a switch (68) beside
            the lamps lever. In the central position of the
            switch, both lamps are OFF and when the switch
            knob is moved to starboard or to port the INNER
            or the OUTER lamp respectively is illuminated.

54.   Signal pistol.- The signal pistol is situated in
            the rear fuselage on the port side of the observer's
            seat and is fired by the observer (see Sect.3.).

F.S/4d

Revised by A.L.14/E

DE-ICING EQUIPMENT

55. **Propeller de-icing.-** On early aeroplanes only, the control (81) for the de-icing of the propeller is mounted on the starboard sill tube and has clearly marked on it the off and on positions. When the knob of the control is rotated in a clockwise direction the speed of the electric-driven ejector pump is increased, and when rotated in a counter-clockwise direction the speed is decreased.

56. **Windscreen de-icing.-** A handpump is fitted below the booster coil switches on the starboard side.

57. **Pressure head heating.-** The heating circuit switch is on the switch block (77) above the compass to starboard.

EMERGENCY EXITS AND EQUIPMENT

58. **Emergency exits.-**

   (i) The pilot's entrance hatch is also used as a parachute exit. To open, pull the bottom caton release lanyard and the airstream will open the hatch and force it into the top catch. The observer's hatch is opened in a similar manner.

   (ii) A further emergency exit is provided on the starboard side of the cockpit by a special window (8) which can be jettisoned. The window is held shut by plunger bolts in catch brackets at each end and is jettisoned by pulling the lever (82) in the centre aft and pushing the window outward.

   (iii) A hatch in the cockpit roof also provides exit. It is hinged on the starboard side and opens outward. The hatch is held shut by plunger bolts, in catch brackets at each end on the port side, and may be opened by first releasing the locking arrangement and then pulling down the handle in the centre. A wire cable is attached to the rear end of the hatch to prevent it from opening too far. On fighter command aeroplanes this hatch has a sliding observation panel. To open pull lever down and back. To lock closed push lever dorward and up. The observer's hood can also be used and opens in a similar manner.

Revised by A.L.14/E   A.P.1721B Vol.I & P.N.Sect.1.

59. **Dinghy equipment & releases** - A multi-seat dinghy is provided in a blow-out stowage built into the trailing edge of the port wing. The dinghy is secured to the interior of the stowage structure by a painter cord of low breaking strength; a pack containing rations, drinking liquid, paddles and recognition devices is provided in the dinghy compartment, connected to the dinghy lifeline by the lanyard provided on the pack.
There are three variations of the Beaufighter dinghy installations:-

   (1) With dinghy type 'H' and operating head type 'G' provision is made for manual operation only by means of a handle outside the fuselage, on the dinghy stowage cover.

   (2) With hinghy type 'H' and operating head type 'H' there are three manual pull offs - (if mod 864 has been incorporated)

      (a) Internally on the port side immediately aft of the pilot's shoulder.

      (b) Internally on the port side, below the astro hatch.

      (c) Externally forward of the leading edge of fin This variation is also provided with an immersion switch for automatic electrical operation of the type 'H' operating head.

   (3) With dinghy type 'L' operated manually and automatically as for (2).

   In addition to the multi-seat dinghy, the following are provided as personal issue. For Pilot: 'K' type dinghy in 'A' type pack. For Observer: 'K' type dinghy in 'C' type pack.

60. **Fuel jettison control.**- By pulling forward the red painted lever (47) on the instrument panel just above the main magneto switches, the fuel in each outer tank (on later aeroplanes the four main tanks) can be jettisoned. The lever controls a pneumatically-operated jettison valve on each tank.

Revised by A.L.14/E

61. **Fire extinguishers**.- The two shielded push-buttons (17) and (18) at the top of the instrument panel, when pressed, release the contents of two fire extinguishers, one in each engine nacelle. A combined impact and gravity switch aft of the fuselage nose to starboard and two flame switches in each engine nacelle provide automatic operation of this extinguisher system. When the undercarriage is retracted the gravity switch is inoperative. Two hand fire-extinguishers are stowed one on the starboard side of the rear fuselage forward of the rear spar, the second on the port side at the junction of the front and rear fuselage.

62. **Axe**.- An axe for cutting a way out of the fuselage in an emergency is stowed on the starboard side of the rear fuselage aft of the front spar.

63. **First-aid outfit**.- A first-aid outfit is stowed on the starboard side of the rear fuselage forward of the rear spar.

64. **Emergency rations**.- Emergency rations are stowed in the rear fuselage at the base of the observer's seat.

65. **Emergency signalling**.- The emergency signalling (on early aeroplanes only) is used only when abandoning the aeroplane and is an entirely independent circuit. There is a switch (77) and a shielded push-button (32) for signalling to the observer. The push-button is to warn the observer to prepare to abandon the aeroplane and the switch to give the final order to abandon. The switch should not be depressed until the warning lamp (33) on the instrument panel lights up informing the pilot that the observer is ready to abandon the aeroplane.

66. **R.3003 or R.3078 Destruction**.- The destruction push switches (71) are in the cockpit on the port side. Both must be pressed simultaneously.

A.P.1721B Vol.I and Pilot's Notes Sect.1

Key to Fig.1

1	Hydraulic power lever
2.	Hydraulic EMERGENCY SELECTOR LEVER
3.	Reflector sight socket
4.	Direct-vision windows (early type)
5.	Reflector sight brackets
6.	Firing button (early type)
7.	Brake lever
8.	EMERGENCY EXIT window
9.	Seat (collapsed position)
10.	Undercarriage control lever
11.	Flap control
12.	Flap position indicator

GENERAL VIEW OF COCKPIT

FIG. 1

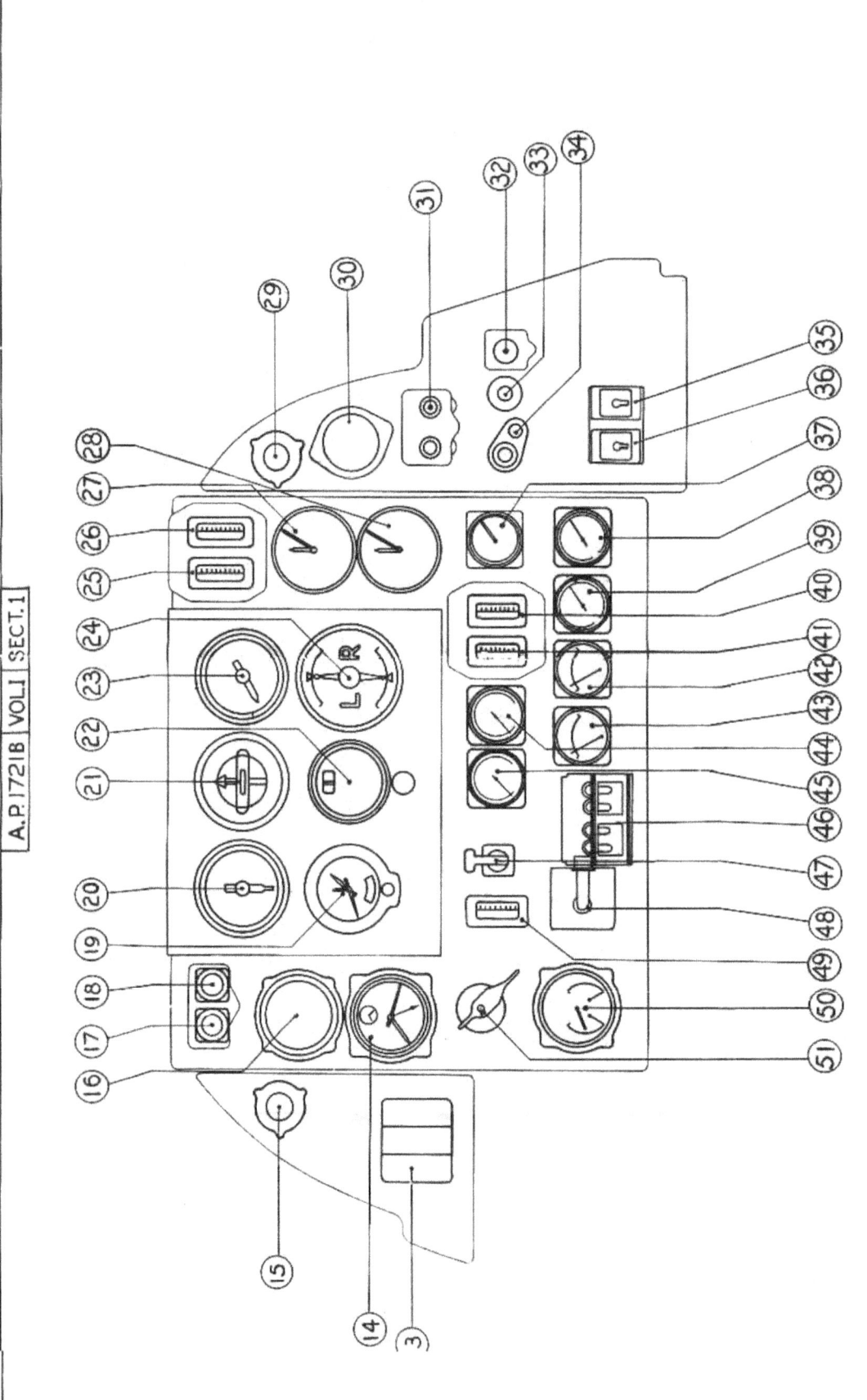

A.F.1721B, Vol.1 and Pilot's Notes Sect.1

Key to Fig.2

13.	Undercarriage and tail wheel position indicators
14.	Clock
15.	Floodlight dimmer switch (port)
16.	Blind approach visual indicator
17.	Fire-extinguisher button, port) shielded
18.	Fire-extinguisher button, starboard)
19.	Altimeter
20.	Airspeed indicator
21.	Artificial horizon
22.	Director indicator
23.	Rate-of-climb indicator
24.	Turn and bank indicator
25.	Oil pressure gauge (port)
26.	Oil pressure gauge (starboard)
27.	R.P.M. indicator (port)
28.	R.P.M. indicator (starboard)
29.	Floodlight dimmer switch (starboard)
30.	Ventilator
31.	Starter button, shielded (port and starboard)
32.	ABANDON AIRCRAFT button, shielded (early aeroplanes)
33.	ABANDON AIRCRAFT lamp (early aeroplanes)
34.	Intercommunication lamp and button
35.	Booster coil switch (starboard)
36.	Booster coil switch (port)
37.	Air temperature gauge
38.	Boost gauge (starboard)
39.	Boost gauge (port)
40.	Fuel pressure gauge (starboard) early aeroplanes
41.	Fuel pressure gauge (port)
42.	Radiator temperature indicator (starboard)
43.	Radiator temperature indicator (port)
44.	Oil temperature gauge (starboard)
45.	Oil temperature gauge (port)
46.	Main magneto switches (port and starboard)
47.	Fuel jettison lever
48.	Undercarriage and tail wheel indicator switch
49.	Vacuum gauge (early aeroplanes)
50.	Pneumatic system triple pressure gauge
51.	Vacuum pump change-over cock control

A.P.1721B, Vol.1 & Pilot's Notes Sect.1

Key to Fig.3

52.	Carburettor cut-out controls (port and starboard)
53.	Fuel cock control (starboard tanks)
54.	Fuel cock control (port tanks)
55.	Suction balance cock control
56.	Carburettor air-intake controls (port and starboard)
57.	Radio remote control (mechanical controller shown)
58.	Oxygen regulator
59.	Fuel contents gauges (port tanks)
60.	Airscrew speed controls (port and starboard)
61.	Throttle levers (port and starboard)
62.	Mixture control
63.	Engine data plate
64.	Engine control friction adjuster
65.	Seat adjusting lever
66.	Cockpit heating control
67.	Landing lamp dipping control
68.	Landing lamp switch
69.	Two-speed supercharger control
70.	Automatic boost control cut-out
71.	R.3003 control

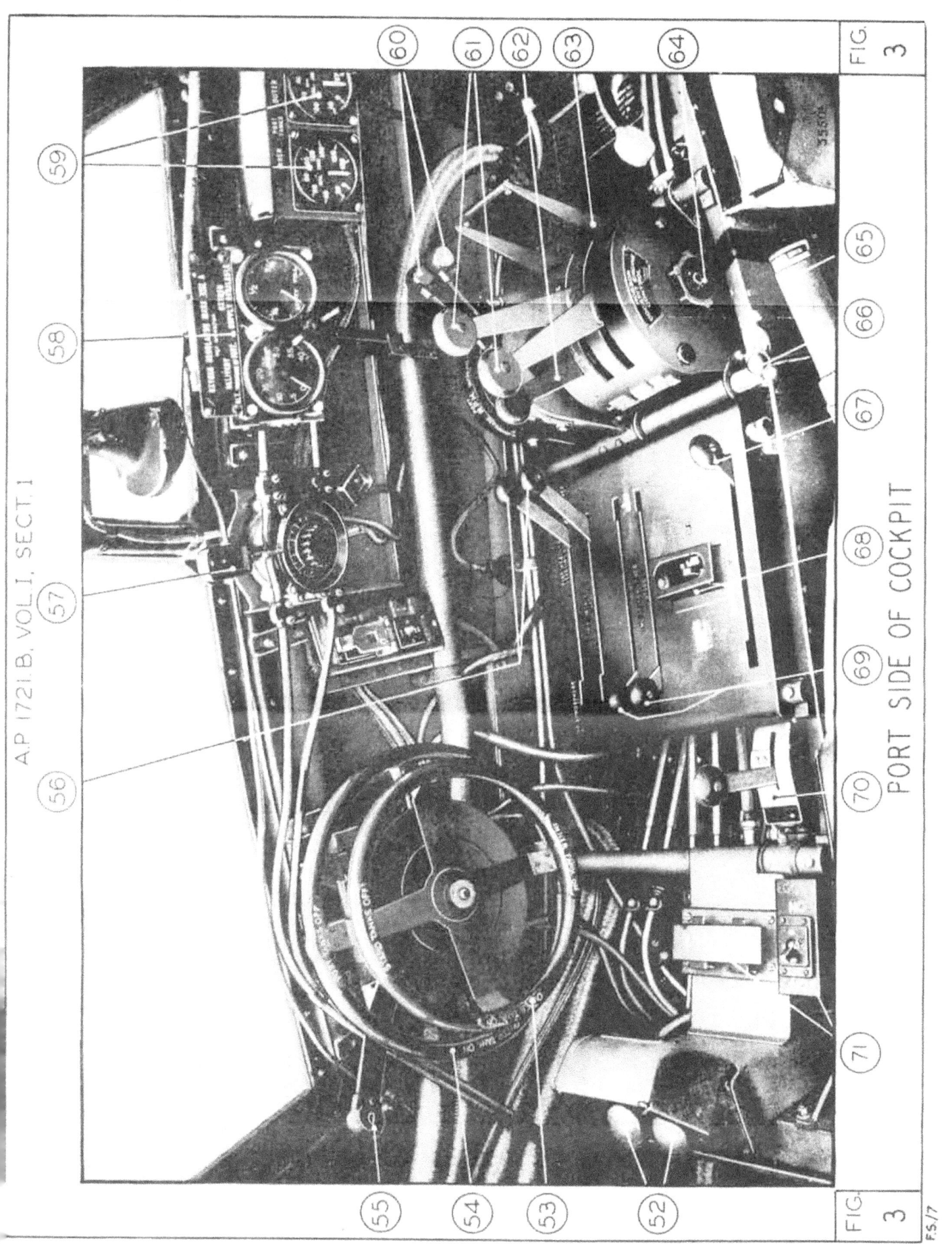

FIG. 3 PORT SIDE OF COCKPIT

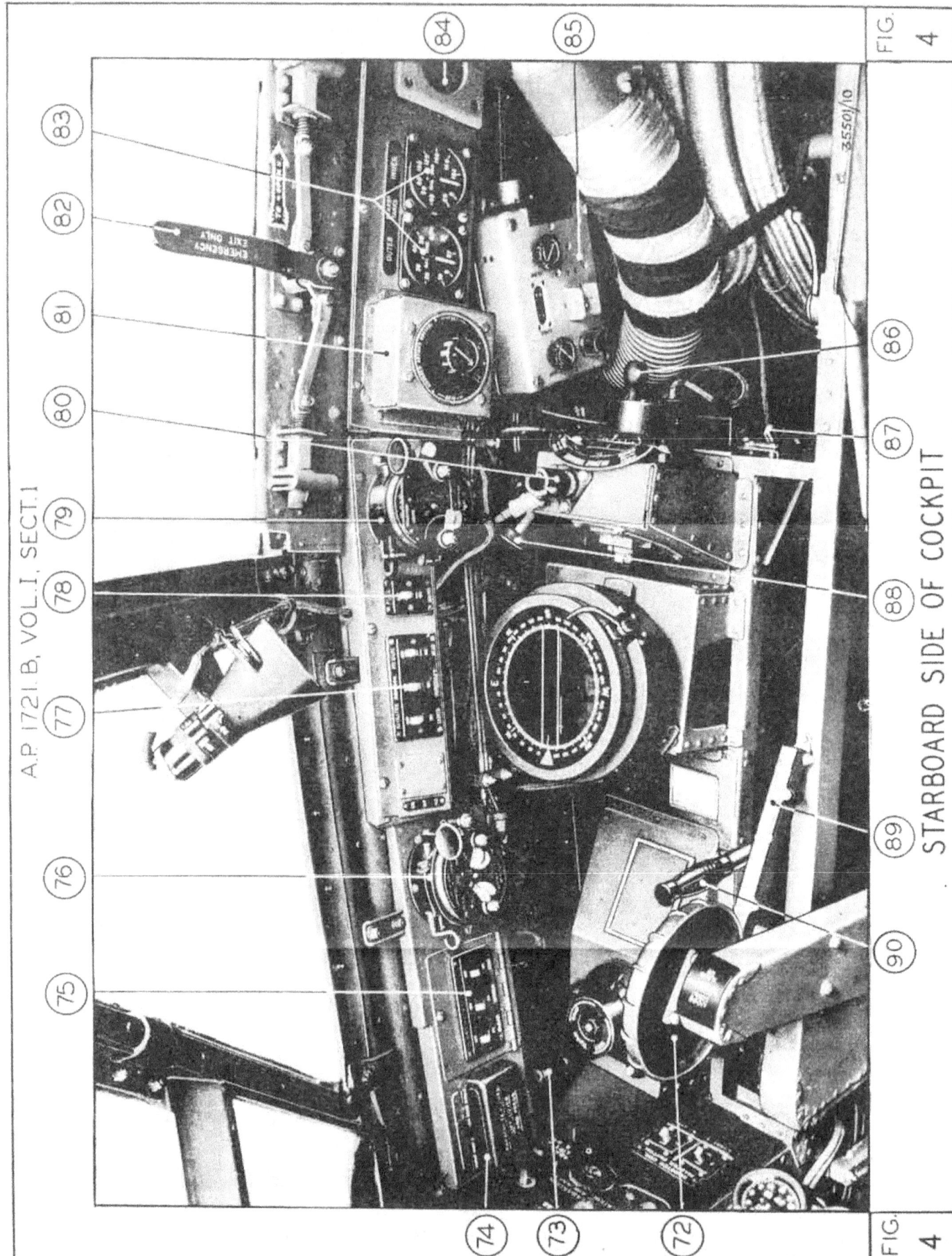

FIG. 4 STARBOARD SIDE OF COCKPIT

A.P.1721B Vol. I and Pilot's Notes Sect.1

Key to fig.4

72. Elevator trimming tab control
73. Rudder trimming tab control
74. Forced landing flare release control
75. Downward identification lamp switches
76. Signalling switchbox for identification lamps
77. Navigation, ABANDON AIRCRAFT and pressure head heating switches
78. Fuel gauge switch
79. Formation-keeping lamp signalling switchbox
80. Oxygen socket
81. Propeller de-icing control
82. EMERGENCY EXIT (starboard) LEVER
83. Fuel contents gauges (starboard tanks)
84. Cine camera footage indicator wedge plate
85. Blind-approach control
86. Aileron trimming tab control
87. Cine camera master switch
88. Microphone-telephone socket
89. Elevator trimming tab position indicator
90. Hydraulic hand pump

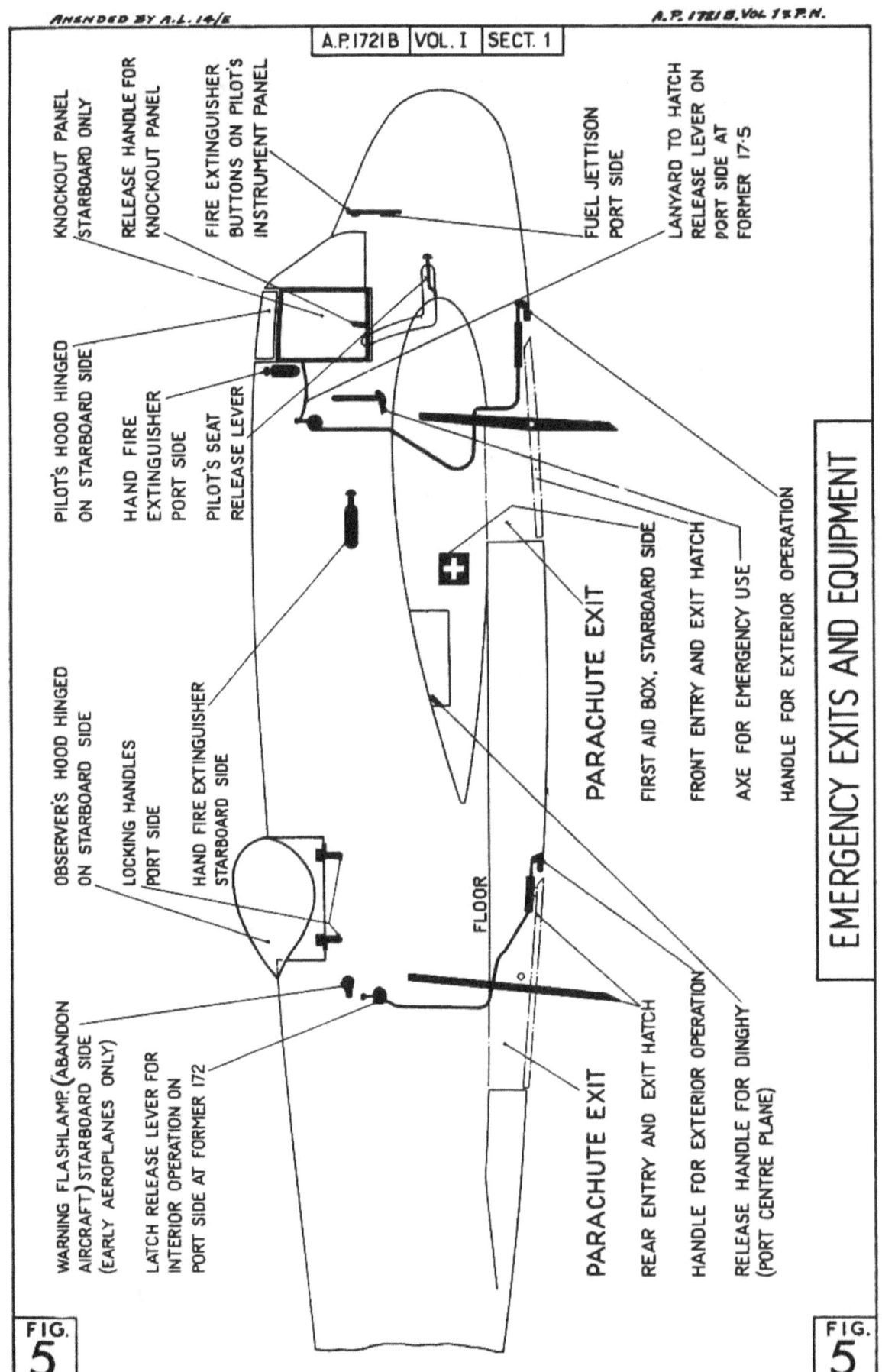

Fig. 5 — Emergency Exits and Equipment

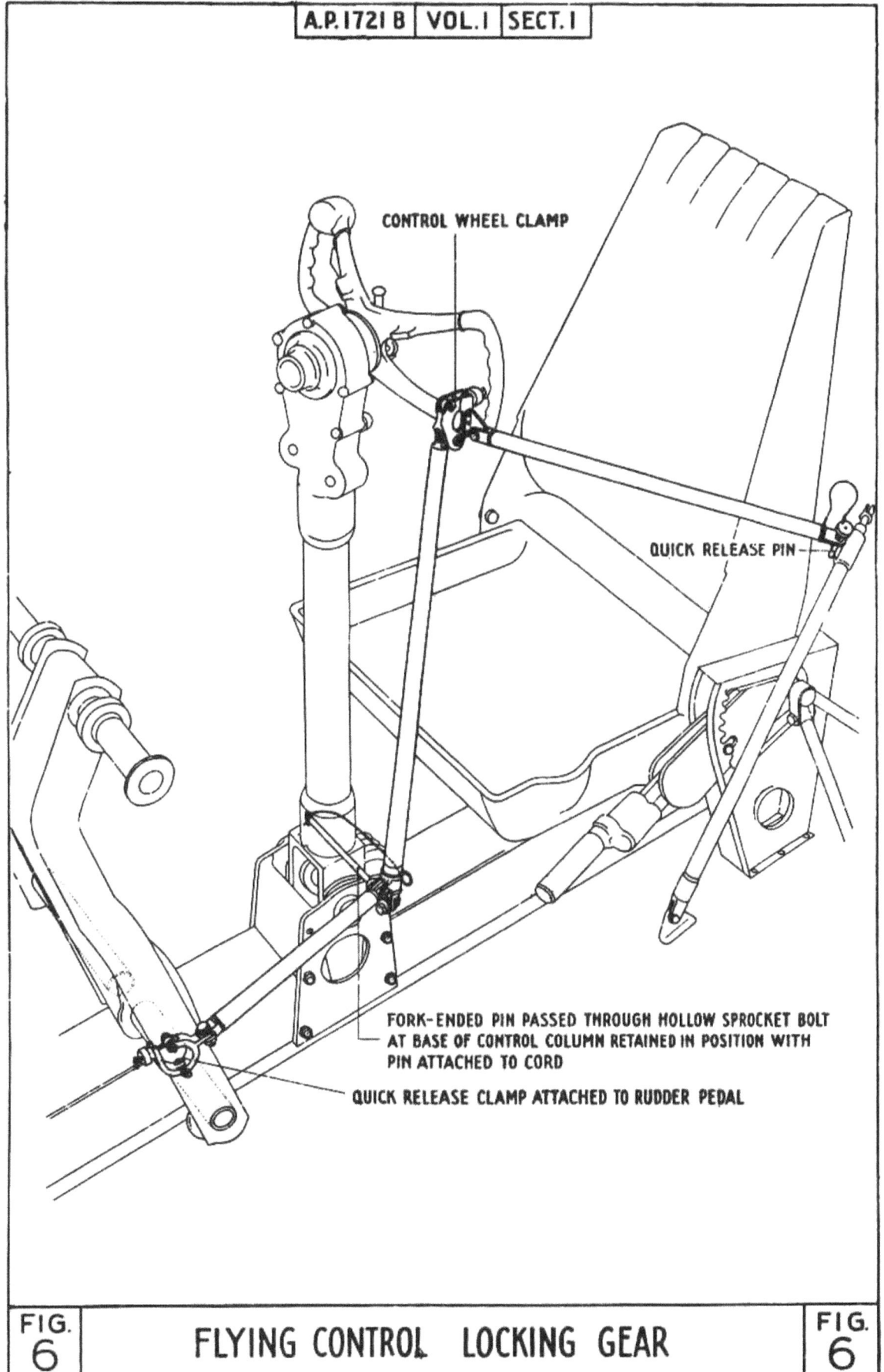

FIG. 6 — FLYING CONTROL LOCKING GEAR

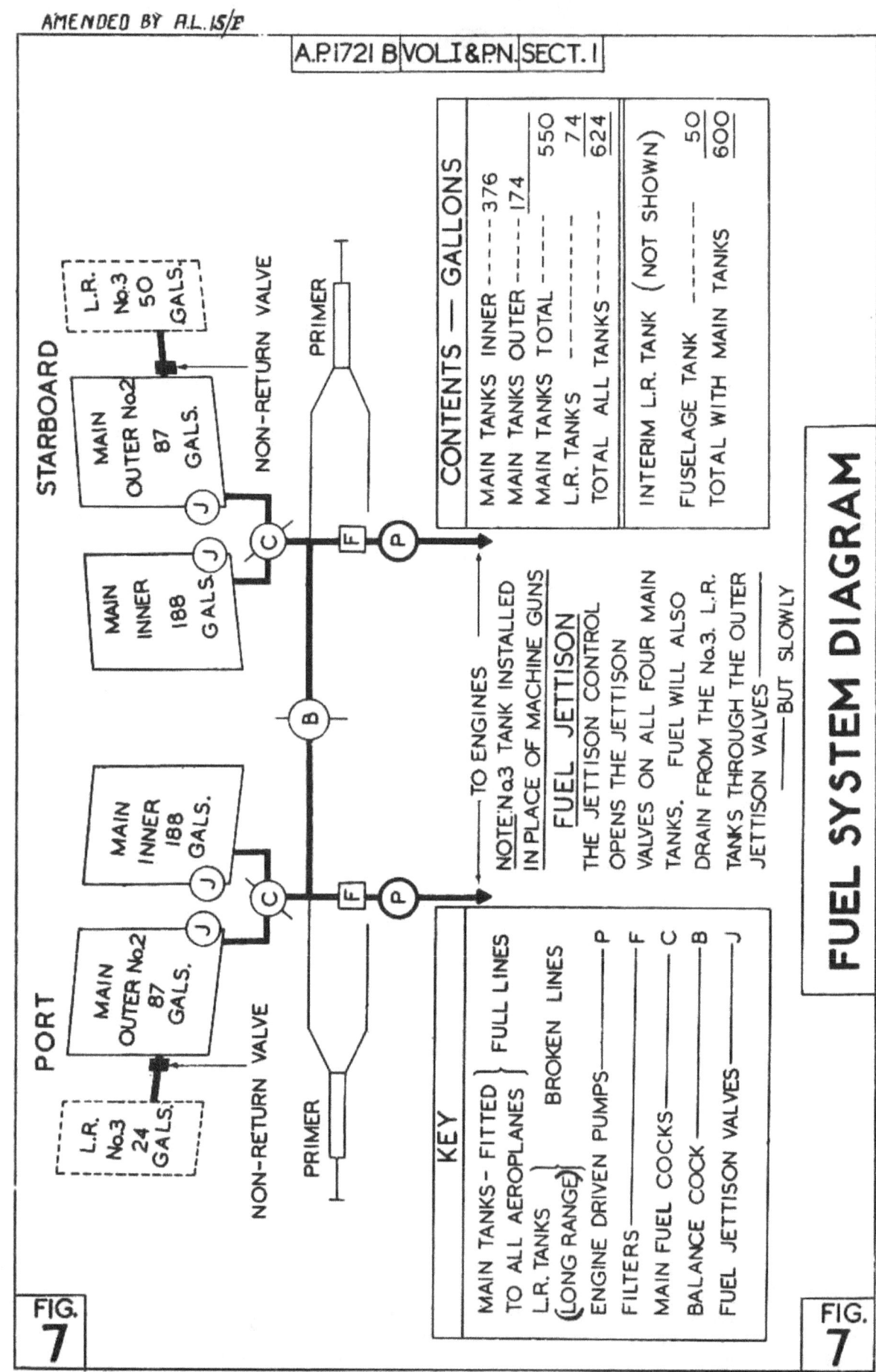

AIR PUBLICATION 1721B

SECTION 2

LIST OF CONTENTS

	Para
Engine Data	1
Position Error Corrections	2
Flying Limitations	3
Preliminaries	4
Starting Engines and Warming Up	5
Testing Engines and Installations	6
Checks before Taxying	7
Check List before Take Off	8
Take Off	9
Climb	10
General Flying	11
Maximum Performance	12
Maximum Range	13
Oil and Fuel Capacities and Consumptions	14
Diving	15
Approach and Landing	16
Mislanding	17
After Landing	18
Engine Failure during Take Off	19
Engine Failure in Flight	20
Undercarriage and Flaps Emergency Operation	21
Ditching	22

Revised by A.L.No.19/G   AIR PUBLICATION 1721B
　　　　　　　　　　　　Volume 1 and
　　　　　　　　　　　　Pilot's Notes.

SECTION 2

Note:- The flying technique outlined in these notes is based on A.P.129 Flying Training Manual Part I, Chapter III and A.P.2095, Pilot's Notes General, to which reference should always be made if further specific information is required.

1.   ENGINE DATA   MERLIN XX
   - (i) Fuel   100 octane only
   - (ii) Oil   See A.P.1464/C.37
   - (iii) The engine limitations are:-

	R.P.M.	BOOST LB/SQ.IN.	TEMP. °C Clnt.	°C Oil
TAKE OFF TO 1,000 FT or 5 MINS	M 3,000	+12		
CLIMBING 1 HR LIMIT	M 2,850 / S 2,850	+ 9 / + 9	125 / 125	90(100) / 90(100)
MAX.RICH CONTINUOUS	M 2,650 / S 2,650	+ 7 / + 7	105(115) / 105(115)	90 / 90
MAX.WEAK CONTINUOUS	M 2,650 / S 2,650	+ 4 / + 4	105(115) / 105(115)	90 / 90
COMBAT 5 MINS LIMIT	M 3,000 / S 3,000	+14* / +16*	125(135) / 125(135)	105 / 105

* Obtainable by pulling boost control cut-out.
Note: Use of the higher temperatures in brackets is permitted for short periods only when operational conditions make the observance of the normal limitations impracticable.

OIL PRESSURE: NORMAL: 60/80 lb/sq.in.
                      MINM : 45   "
MINM.TEMP. FOR TAKE-OFF: OIL : 15°C
                              COOLANT 60°C

Revised by A.L.No.19/G

2. POSITION ERROR CORRECTIONS

At 19,000 lb. the corrections are as follows:-

From to	130 150	150 170	170 190	190 210	210 230	230 255	255 280	m.p.h. I.A.S.
Add	6	4	2	-				
Subtract					-	2	4	6

3. FLYING LIMITATIONS

(i) Maximum permissible weights are:-

For take-off, all forms of flying and landing: 21,000 lb.

(ii) The aircraft is designed for the duties of a long range reconnaissance fighter and intentional spinning and aerobatics are not permitted.

(iii) Maximum permissible speeds in m.p.h. I.A.S. are:-

Diving 400
Undercarriage starting to lower 170
Flaps lowering 150 (200 if mod 47 is incorporated)
Undercarriage down 150
Flaps fully down 135

4. PRELIMINARIES

On entering the cockpit, set or check the following

(i) Hydraulic power lever — ON

(ii) Undercarriage lever — DOWN

(iii) Switch on the indicator to confirm that the undercarriage is locked.

Amended in Vol. 1 by A.L.No.25   A.P.1721B Sect.2
Amended in P.Ns. by A.L/J

5.   STARTING ENGINES AND WARMING UP

   (i)   Set or check the following:

          Balance cock   - OFF

          Fuel cocks   - Inner tanks ON

          Throttles   - ½ inch open

          Mixture control   - NORMAL

          Propeller speed controls - Fully forward

          Superchargers   - "M" ratio

          Carburettor air intake   - Cold

   (ii)   Instruct the ground crew to work the priming pump
          for the induction system until the suction and
          delivery pipes are primed. This may be judged by a
          sudden increase in resistance to the plunger. High
          volatile fuel (Stores ref.No.34A/111) should be
          used, if an external priming connection is fitted, at
          temperatures below freezing.

   (iii) Switch ON the ignition and booster coil.

   (iv)   Press the starter button for each engine in turn,
          for periods of not more than 20 seconds with a
          wait of 30 seconds between each attempt. The
          ground crew will prime the induction system of each
          engine while it is being turned; they should start
          after the following number of strokes:

          Air temperature °C: +30   +20   +10   0   -10   -20

          Normal fuel: 3   4   7   12

          High volatile fuel: 4   8   18

          If K40 (40 c.c.) pumps are fitted divide strokes by
          four giving an incomplete stroke where necessary.

   (vi)   It may be necessary to continue priming after the
          engine has fired, until it picks up on the carbure-
          ttor.

   (vii) As soon as the engine is firing steadily, switch
          off the booster coil. The ground crew will screw
          down the priming pumps.

   (viii) Run each engine slowly for half a minute, then warm
          up at 1,000 r.p.m. until the oil inlet temperature
          is at least 15°C and the coolant temperature above
          60°C.

6. TESTING ENGINES AND INSTALLATIONS

   While warming up:

   (i) Check hydraulic pressure on both engines: 600 lb/sq.in.

   (ii) Check suction of blind flying vacuum pumps (if gauge is fitted). Use the pumps alternately, changing over between each flight.

   (iii) Check fuel pressure (6 to 8 lb/sq.in) if gauge or indicator is fitted.

   (iv) Instruct the ground crew to make certain that both EMERGENCY escape HATCHES are correctly fastened.

   After warming up, for each engine in turn:

   (v) At zero boost (but in rich mixture) exercises and check operation of the two-speed superchargers.

   (vi) At zero boost exercise and check the operation of the propeller.

   (vii) Open the throttle fully and check take-off boost, r.p.m. and oil pressure.

   (viii) Test each magnetic is turn at +9 lb/sq.in. boost; if propeller is constant speeding at this boost, close throttle slightly until a slight drop in r.p.m. is noted and then test. The drop should not exceed 150 r.p.m.

7. CHECKS BEFORE TAXYING

   (i) See that the ground crew remove and hold up the undercarriage safety links and stow them in the aircraft.

   (ii) Check tail-wheel lock (if fitted) - unlocked

   (iii) Brake pressure - minimum - 100 lb/sq.in.

8. CHECK LIST BEFORE TAKE-OFF

   H - Hydraulic power lever   - ON

   T - Trimming tabs   - Elevator; One inch nose down on indicator
                                  Aileron: NEUTRAL
                                  Rudder: NEUTRAL

   "Boost control cut-out - pulled"

Revised by A.L.No.19/G A.P.1721B Vol.I & P.N., Sect.2

M - Mixture	- NORMAL
P - Pitch	- Fire (fully forward)
F - Fuel	- Check contents of tanks and cocks settings to INNER TANKS ON
F - Flaps	- Up
Superchargers	- "M" ratio
Tail wheel lock (if fitted)	- Locked (after turning into wind)

Note: It is recommended that the flaps should not be used for take-off. Their use (at $15°$ to $20°$ down) considerably increases the tendency to swing and has only a very slight effect on the length of the take-off run.

9.   TAKE OFF

(i) Open the throttles slightly to start moving, turn into wind, steady the aircraft by rudder, running straight forward a few feet to ensure that the tail wheel is straight.

(ii) Open the throttles to the TAKE-OFF position, taking only two or three second in doing so (slowly for the first inch or so, to ensure that both engines are responding evenly.)

(iii) It is essential to raise the tail as early as possible. It will be found that there is a strong tendency to swing to port, but this may be corrected by coarse use of the rudder. Hold the nose in a constant attitude and let the aircraft fly itself off. Do not try to pull it off the ground too early by depressing the tail.

(iv) Raise the undercarriage when safely airborne, the thumb catch on the operating lever should not be disengaged; it does not lock the lever unless the wheels are on the ground.

(v) The safety speed at take-off power is 160 m.p.h. I.A.S.

(vi) Set hydraulic power lever OFF to prevent pumps overheatir

10.   CLIMB

Climb at about 150 m.p.h. I.A.S.

Revised by A.L.No.19/G

11. **GENERAL FLYING**

 (i) The elevator tab control is designed to assist manoeuvring and recovery from dives, and the control wheel is in a convenient position for this purpose, but the tab control must be used very slowly and carefully because it is powerful and sudden use causes heavy stresses in the structure.

 (ii) Stability

  (a) <u>Unmodified aircraft</u>:- At high speeds the aircraft is just stable in pitch, but at lower speeds, when climbing or approaching to land, it becomes unstable and cannot be flown "hands off" for more than a few seconds at a time. The instability is more pronounced when the flaps are lowered. The lateral stability is about neutral.

  (b) <u>Modified aircraft</u> with dihedral tail and weight on control column.- The aircraft is longitudinally stable in level flight down to 140 m.p.h. I.A.S. On the climb, it is neutrally stable or slightly stable at the speed for maximum rate of climb. On the glide, the aircraft is stable both with flaps and undercarriage up and down.

 (iii) Change of trim

   Flaps down   - nose goes down.

   Undercarriage down   - nose goes down slightly

 (iv) <u>Stalling</u>.- The weight at take-off with full tanks will be about 20,400 lb. With outer tanks empty and half the ammunition expended the weight is about 19,500 lb. and the stalling speed given below apply to this weight.

  (a) <u>Undercarriage and flaps up</u>.- The aircraft stalls at approximately 100/105 m.p.h. I.A.S., and if the control column is held back the nose and one wing drop sharply. The wings may pass the vertical if there is any delay in pushing the control column forward.

  (b) <u>Undercarriage and flaps down</u>.- With the engines throttled right back the stalling speed is approximately 80/85 m.p.h. I.A.S. The stall is usually preceded by a slight pitching oscillation. The nose and one wing usually drop sharply at the stall, especially if the throttles are slightly open.

Revised by A.L.No.19/G   A.P.1721B Vol.I & P.N. Sect.2

    (v)   <u>Flying at reduced airspeeds</u>. When flying in conditions of bad visibility near the ground, open cockpit side windows.

        (a) Do not lower the undercarriage unless to make a landing on safe ground.

        (b) Speed may be safely reduced to about 130 m.p.h. I.A.S. provided that no rapid manoeuvre is attempted.

        (c) In extreme cases flaps should be lowered about $15° - 20°$, and speed reduced even as low as 120 m.p.h. I.A.S.

        (d) Engine speed should be maintained at about 2,600 r.p.m. so that ample power is available if the throttles are opened suddenly in an emergency.

12.   <u>MAXIMUM PERFORMANCE</u>

    (i)   Climbing

        (a) The speeds for maximum rate of climb are:

            140 m.p.h. I.A.S. from S.L. to 18,000 ft.
            135   "   "   from 18,000 to 23,000 ft.
            130   "   "   above 23,000 ft.

        (b) Change to S gear when the boost has dropped to +6 lb/sq.in.

    (ii)   Combat

        Use S gear if +10 lb/sq.in. boost cannot be maintained, in M gear (with boost control cut-out pulled).

13.   <u>MAXIMUM RANGE</u>

    (i)   The recommended speed for greatest range is:-

        170 m.p.h. I.A.S. (160 m.p.h. I.A.S. If undercarriage doors are not fitted)

    (ii)   Fly in weak mixture in M gear at maximum obtainable boost not exceeding +4 lb/sq.in. and adjust r.p.m., which may be as low as 1,800 r.p.m., to give the recommended speed. At low r.p.m. observer should check generator charging by warning light (if fitted), ammeter or voltmeter.

    (iii)   If the recommended speed cannot be maintained in M gear at 2,600 r.p.m., change to S gear.

Revised by A.L.No.19/G

- (iii) If the recommended speed cannot be maintained in M gear at 2,600 r.p.m. change to S gear.

- (iv) At low altitudes, if 1,800 r.p.m. at +4 lb/sq.in. boost gives a higher speed than that recommended it is more economical to fly at this speed than to reduce speed by reducing boost.

14. OIL & FUEL CAPACITIES & CONSUMPTIONS

- (i) Oil: The effective capacity of each tank is 17 gallons (total 34)

- (ii) Fuel: The effective capacities are:-

Main tanks - inner	- 376	gallons
Main tanks - outer	- 174	"
	550 550	"
Long range tanks	74	"
Total effective capacity	624	"
Fuselage tank (interim)	50	"
Total with fuselage tank	600	"

- (iii) Fuel consumptions

    Total consumptions in gallons her hour are approximately:-

    (a) In weak misture

Boost	R.P.M.		
lb/sq.in.	2650	2300	2000
+4	114	102	94
+2	106	94	86
0	96	86	78
-2	86	78	70
-4	76	68	62

    (b) In rich mixture

Boost	R.P.M.		
lb/sq.in.	3000	2850	2650
+12	230	-	-
+ 9	200	190	-
+ 7	-	-	160

15. DIVING

- (i) Leave the propeller speed control set to give cruising r.p.m.

Revised by A.L.No.19/G   A.P. 1721B Vol.I & P.N. Sect.2.

(ii) The aircraft should be trimmed into, and out of, the dive and on recovery, which should be as gradual as possible, especially at high weights, the elevator trim control must be used slowly and carefully (see para. 11/i)).

16. APPROACH AND LANDING

  (i) Stability.- The stability differs markedly according as the aircraft has or has not been modified. See Para. 11(ii). On unmodified aircraft the instability on the glide is increased when the flaps are lowered and it is recommended that they should not be lowered until the end of the last turn, especially at night.

  (ii) Preliminary approach.- Undercarriage lowering may be begun at 170 m.p.h. I.A.S. and flap lowering at 150 m.p.h. I.A.S. Speed must be reduced to 135 m.p.h. I.A.S. as soon as possible after the undercarriage is fully down, and before the flaps are fully down.

  (iii) Checks before landing.- H.U.M.P. Supercharger and Flaps.

  H - Hydraulic power lever   - ON
  U - Undercarriage   - DOWN
  M - Mixture   - NORMAL
  P - Propeller   - Propeller speed controls fully forward
      Supercharger   - M ratio
  F - Flaps   - Fully DOWN

  Tailwheel lock (if fitted) - locked

  (iv) Recommended speeds for final approach at 19,500 lb. in m.p.h. I.A.S. are:-

	Flaps down	Flaps up
Engine assisted	100	120
Glide	115	135

  Note: Turns during a gliding approach should only be executed at 5 to 10 m.p.h. above these speeds and turns with steep bank, or near the ground, should not be attempted.

17. MISLANDING

  If baulked the aircraft will climb easily at climbing r.p.m. and boost with flaps and undercarriage down but note:-

Revised by A.L.No.19/G

    (i) The undercarriage should be raised immediately

    (ii) Climb at 120 m.p.h. I.A.S. and raise flaps at not less than 300 to 400 ft. There will be no tendency to sink at this speed.

    (iii) Should one engine fail with flaps down fully, make the best landing possible.

18. **AFTER LANDING**

    (i) Raise flaps and unlock tail-wheel lock (if fitted). before taxying.

    (ii) Leave hydraulic power lever - ON

    (iii) Run engine at 800 to 900 r.p.m. for two minutes, then pull slow-running cut-outs to stop engines. When they have stopped switch off ignition and all electrical services; turn off fuel cocks.

    (iv) See that the undercarriage safety locking pins are replaced.

    (v) <u>Oil dilution</u>.- See A.P.2095

    The correct dilution periods for this aircraft are.-
    1 minute down to $-10^\circ C$.
    2 minutes below this temperature.

EMERGENCIES

19. **ENGINE FAILURE DURING TAKE-OFF**

    (i) If it is necessary to raise the undercarriage while still on the ground, the thumb catch on the undercarriage operating lever must first be released (see Section 1).

    (ii) If safety speed has been attained, throttle back to the RATED gate and the, climb at about 140 m.p.h. I.A.S.

    (iii) Set the propeller speed control of the dead engine fully back. This will give the least possible drag.

20. **ENGINE FAILURE IN FLIGHT**

    (i) On one engine at a weight of 20,4000 lbs. height can be maintained at cruising boost and r.p.m. and rudder control is adequate down to about 125 m.p.h. I.A.S. For continuous flight on one engine, speed should be about 140 m.p.h.I.A.S.

Note: The throttle should <u>never</u> be so far opened that full rudder is required to keep the aircraft straight. Set the propeller speed control of the dead engine fully back.

(ii) If flying by instrument it is advisable first to close both throttles and then open the live engine up slowly.

(iii) <u>Correct speeds for approach on one engine</u>:

    (a) Before flaps are lowered: 130 m.p.h. I.A.S.

    (b) After lowering flaps: 115 m.p.h. I.A.S.

21. UNDERCARRIAGE AND FLAPS EMERGENCY OPERATION

(i) Never use the emergency system unless the normal engine pump system has failed, then use the hand-pump emergency system as follows:-

    (a) Set hydraulic power lever - OFF
        Set emergency selector - ON
        Then pump.

    Note: The undercarriage and flaps will come down together if the flaps and undercarriage levers remain either UP or DOWN (<u>if MOD.853 has not been incorporated the flap lever must be left UP or set DOWN</u>). They cannot be raised by means of the emergency system.

    (b) After incorporation of MOD.853.- to lower the undercarriage only, set flap lever - Neutral. (On later aircraft an interlock does this when the emergency selector is set to ON). The flaps can be lowered subsequently by setting the flap lever - DOWN.

(ii) Should the emergency system fail try the hand pump through the normal system as follows:-

    Set emergency selector   - OFF
    Set hydraulic power lever   - ON
    Set flaps and undercarriage levers as required.

The flaps and undercarriage can be raised as well as lowered by this system.

Revised by A.L.No.19/G

22. DITCHING

See A.P.2095 and note:

(i) Flaps should be set 30° down.

(ii) Should the undercarriage be down an attempt should be made to raise if (if there is time) or in any case to unlock it, if necessary with the hand pump through the normal pipe lines, i.e. emergency selector - OFF, power lever - ON undercarriage selector - UP.

(iii) The deceleration is likely to be severe and much water may come over the nose and into the cockpit. The aircraft may swerve.

Issued with A.L.14/E.   A.P.1721B. Vol.I & P.N.Sect.2.

PARACHUTE DRILL — BEAUFIGHTER I & VI.

1. (a) **PILOT.** Pilot will give the order to prepare to jump over the inter-comm to the operator and give "May Day" and fixing transmission on R.T. (if over sea).

   (b) Listen for acknowledging "Preparing to jump" from operator. Upon receipt of this he should prepare to jump himself as follows:-

   (c) Release Sutton harness and check parachute quick release for safe.

   (d) Reach back with left hand and pull emergency release lever forward.

   (e) Jettison petrol.

   (f) Trim aircraft for glide with flaps down.

2. (a) Upon receipt of "Ready to jump" from operator give the order "Jump" and at the same time switch off the engines.

   (b) Collapse seat, pull out intercommunication plug and oxygen bayonet.

   (c) Reach back, grasp overhead hand rails with both hands and pull himself out of seat.

   (d) Abandon aircraft by dropping through emergency hatch. If this is impossible, leave through starboard exit.

1. (a) **RADIO OPERATOR.** On receipt of the order 'Prepare to jump' from pilot the operator should reply "Preparing to jump".

   (b) Switch on all cockpit lights in rear of aircraft and set I.F.F. to No. 3. position (if over sea).

   (c) Revolve seat from facing forward position to facing aft position.

   (d) Release Sutton harness and remove oxygen bayonet from socket.

   (e) Attach parachute and dinghy to harness and check quick release.

   (f) Vacate seat and take up position aft of hatch facing forward.

   (g) Push emergency exit lever forward and at the same time pull up by cable provided.

2. (a) Inform pilot "Ready to jump".

   (b) On receipt of order to jump pull out intercommunication plug and jump.

   Note "A". If time and the attitude of the aircraft permit, the radio operator should go forward to join the pilot and then make his escape through the front hatch. This front hatch is sometimes difficult to open and the radio operator should go forward to operate it for the pilot unless the aircraft has to be abandoned at short notice.

   Note "B". If the pilot finds his intercommunication is broken he will send a succession of J's on morse light intercommunication system meaning Jump. Operator will reply with J's meaning "I am about to jump".

   Note "C". Pilots and radio operators must test both escape hatches once a week.

3rd Edition　　　　　　　　　　　　　　　　　　　A.P. 1721H—P.N.

PILOT'S NOTES
FOR
BEAUFIGHTER TFX
TWO HERCULES XVII OR XVIII ENGINES

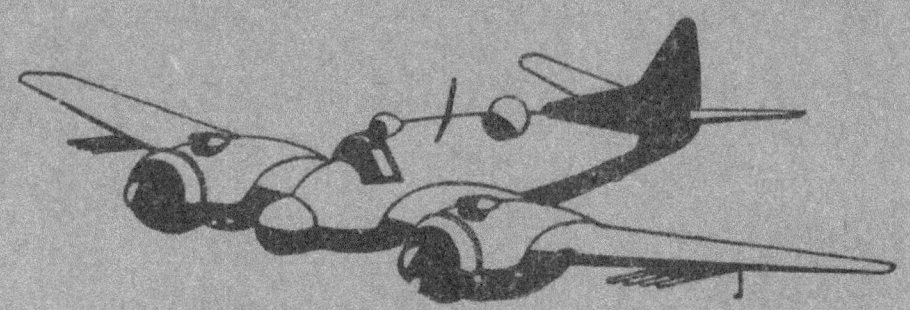

PREPARED BY DIRECTION OF THE MINISTER OF SUPPLY

J. S. Franks.

PROMULGATED BY ORDER OF THE AIR COUNCIL

W. B. Brown

"CROWN COPYRIGHT. REPRODUCED BY PERMISSION OF HER MAJESTY'S STATIONERY OFFICE"

AMENDMENTS

Amendment lists will be issued as necessary and will be gummed for affixing to the inside back cover of these notes.

Each amendment list will include all current amendments and will, where applicable, be accompanied by gummed slips for sticking in the appropriate places in the text.

Incorporation of an amendment list must be certified by inserting date of incorporation and initials below.

A.L. NO.	INITIALS	DATE	A.L. NO.	INITIALS	DATE
1			7		
2			8		
3			9		
4			10		
5			11		
6			12		

NOTES TO USERS

THIS publication is divided into five parts: Descriptive, Handling, Operating Data, Emergencies, and Illustrations. Part I gives only a brief description of the controls with which the pilot should be acquainted.

These Notes are complementary to A.P. 2095 Pilot's Notes General and assume a thorough knowledge of its contents. All pilots should be in possession of a copy of A.P. 2095 (see A.M.O. A93/43).

Words in capital letters indicate the actual markings on the controls concerned.

Additional copies may be obtained by the Station Publications Officer by application on Form 294A, in duplicate, to Command headquarters for onward transmission to A.P.F.S., 81 Fulham Road, S.W.3 (see A.M.O. A1114/44). The number of this publication must be quoted in full—A.P. 1721H—P.N.

Comments and suggestions should be forwarded through the usual channels to the Air Ministry (D.T.F.).

BEAUFIGHTER TFX

AIR MINISTRY
March 1946

AIR PUBLICATION 1721H—P.N.
Pilot's Notes

BEAUFIGHTER TF MK. X
PILOT'S NOTES
3rd Edition

These notes supersede all previous issues which covered this mark of aircraft

LIST OF CONTENTS

PART I—DESCRIPTIVE

INTRODUCTION

FUEL AND OIL SYSTEMS
Para.

Fuel Tanks	1
Fuel cocks	2
Fuel contents gauges	3
Fuel pressure warning lights	4
Priming system	5
Oil system	6

MAIN SERVICES

Hydraulic system	7
Pneumatic system	8
Electrical system	9

AIRCRAFT CONTROLS

Flying controls	10
Flying controls locking gear	11
Trimming tab controls	12
Undercarriage	13
Undercarriage position indicators	14
Flaps control	15
Flaps position indicator	16
Wheel brakes	17

ENGINE CONTROLS

	Para.
Throttle controls	18
Mixture control	19
Propeller controls	20
Supercharger controls	21
Cowling gills controls	22
Carburettor air intake heat controls	23
Ignition switches	24
Engine starting controls	25
Slow running cut-out controls	26

OPERATIONAL CONTROLS

Torpedo sight	27
Torpedo depth setting control	28
Torpedo and bomb master selector switches ...	29
Bomb fuzing switches	30
Torpedo and bomb firing pushbutton	31
R/P switches	32
R/P firing pushbutton	33
R/P rails jettison control	34
Gun sight	35
Gun firing pushbutton	36

OTHER CONTROLS

Cockpit heating and ventilating controls ...	37
Cockpit lighting	38
Pilot's seat collapsing lever	39
Windscreen wiper and de-icing controls	40
R.I. compass	41

PART II—HANDLING

Management of the fuel system	42
Preliminaries	43
Starting the engines and warming up	44
Testing the engines and services	45
Taxying	46
Check list before take-off	47
Take-off	48
Climbing	49
General flying	50

PART II—HANDLING—cont.

	Para.
Stalling	51
Diving	52
Approach and landing	53
Mislanding	54
Beam Approach	55
After landing	56

PART III—OPERATING DATA

Engine data: Hercules XVII and XVIII	57
Position error corrections	58
Flying limitations	59
Maximum performance	60
Maximum range	61
Fuel capacities and consumptions	62

PART IV—EMERGENCIES

Engine failure after take-off	63
Engine failure in flight	64
Feathering	65
Unfeathering	66
Fuel jettisoning	67
Undercarriage and flaps-emergency operation	68
Single engine landing	69
Fire-extinguishers	70
Torpedo, bomb, R/P rails and drop tank jettisoning	71
Parachute exits	72
Crash exits	73
Dinghies	74
Ditching	75

PART V—ILLUSTRATIONS

	Fig.
Cockpit—general view	1
Cockpit—port side	2
Cockpit—starboard side	3

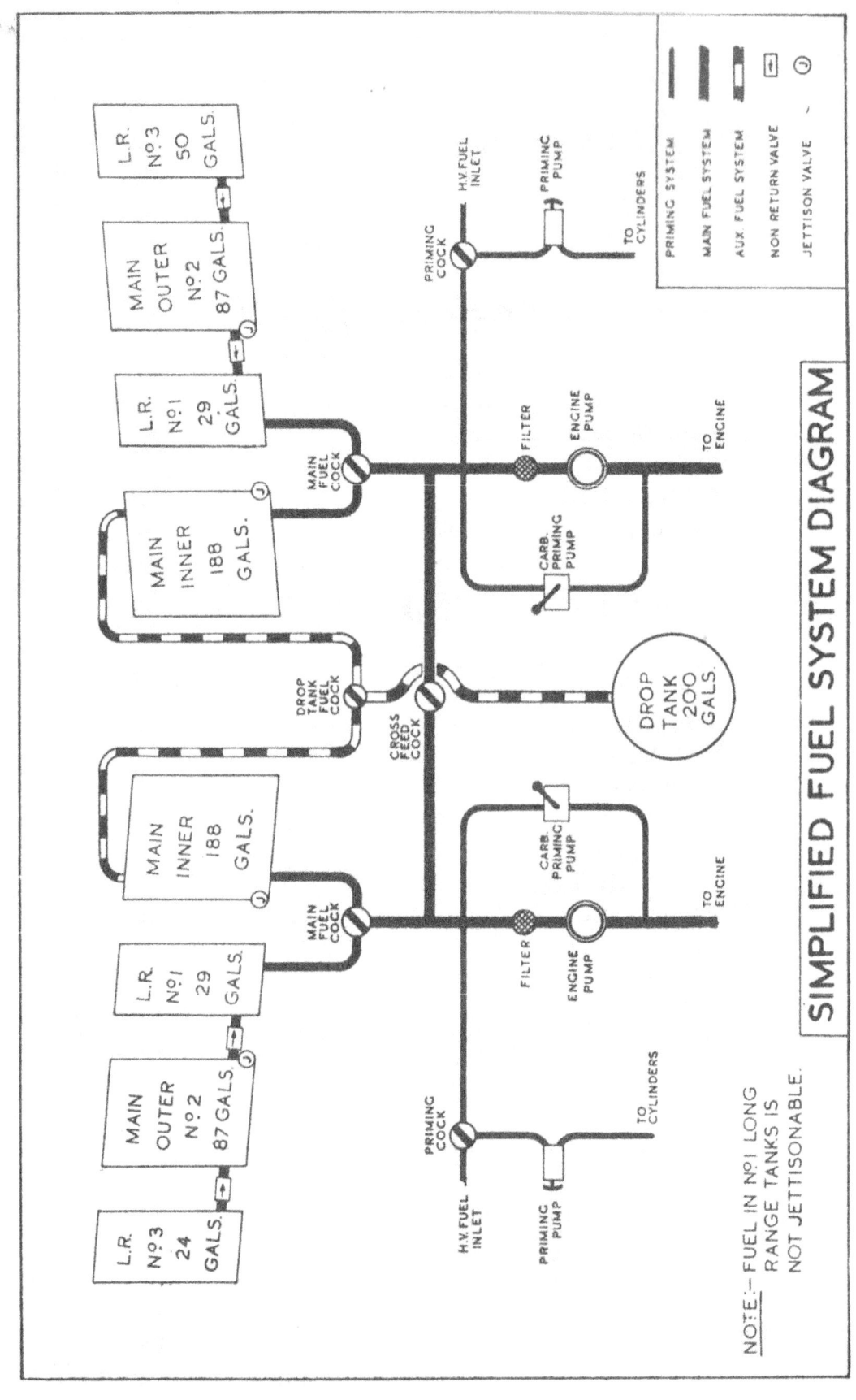

A.P. 1721H—P.N.
Pilot's Notes

PART I

DESCRIPTIVE

INTRODUCTION

The Beaufighter T.F. Mk. X is a long-range low-altitude torpedo-carrying fighter. It is powered by two Hercules XVII or XVIII engines driving three-bladed fully feathering Hydromatic propellers.
A variety of external stores may be carried.

NOTE.—Unless otherwise specified these notes apply only to aircraft which incorporate modifications T.361, T.375 and T.376, and which are fitted with " paddle bladed " propellers.

FUEL AND OIL SYSTEMS

1. **Fuel tanks**

(i) Fuel is carried in four main self-sealing tanks, two in each wing.

(ii) Later aircraft have four additional self-sealing tanks which, in effect, form enlarged outer main tanks. Aircraft which have these additional tanks do not carry the wing machine guns. The tanks in each wing are interconnected by a cross feed pipe and cock.

(iii) A 200-gallon non-selfsealing drop tank can be carried on the torpedo rack. The tank is pressurised and the flow of fuel from it is controlled by a cock (32), marked ON—DROP TANK—OFF, which is fitted below the main fuel cocks. There is an air pressure gauge (43) forward of the cock lever. When the tank is full this gauge should read $2\frac{1}{2}$ lb./sq. in ; as the tank empties pressure will fall gradually to 2 lb./sq. in.
The fuel from the drop tank is fed into the tops of the main inner tanks above the fuel level and cannot, therefore, feed the engines directly. The drop tank can be jettisoned in emergency or when operationally necessary, *see* para. 71.

PART I—DESCRIPTIVE

(iv) The capacities are as follows:

	Permanent tanks galls.	Aux. tanks galls.	Max. capacity galls.
MAIN SUPPLY			
Inner wing tanks (2 × 188) ...	376	—	—
Outer wing tanks (2 × 87) ...	174		550
LONG RANGE WING TANKS (24+29+29+50)	132		132
FUSELAGE DROP TANK (1 × 200)		200	200
Totals	682	200	882

2. **Fuel cocks**

   The two main fuel cocks (30) marked BOTH TANKS OFF—OUTER TANK ON—INNER TANK ON, are mounted on the left-hand cockpit wall level with the pilot's elbow.

   When both cocks are set to OUTER TANK ON or INNER TANK ON, the engines are fed from their respective wing tanks.

   A crossfeed cock (31) marked SUCTION BALANCE, is mounted outboard of the two main fuel cocks; it enables either engine to be fed from the tanks in the opposite wing.

3. **Fuel contents gauges**

   Eight fuel contents gauges are provided for the wing tanks; they will only indicate when the electrical services switch, which is linked with the ignition switches, is ON.

   The gauges (3) for the port main inner and outer tanks are mounted on the left-hand cockpit wall, above the engine controls box. The gauges (54) for the starboard main inner and outer tanks are mounted on the right

PART I—DESCRIPTIVE

hand cockpit wall above and behind the aileron trimming tab control, while the long-range tank gauges (55) are on the right-hand cockpit wall behind the pilot's right shoulder.

NOTE.—There is no contents gauge for the drop tank.

4. **Fuel pressure warning lights**

   Two fuel pressure warning lights (23) are mounted on the bottom right-hand side of the instrument panel. They come on whenever fuel pressure at the carburettors falls appreciably below normal.

5. **Priming system**

   A Ki-gass priming pump is fitted in each engine nacelle. A three-way cock next to the pump permits high volatility fuel to be drawn from an outside source for priming at air temperatures below freezing.

6. **Oil system**

   (i) Oil is supplied from two self-sealing tanks, each of 24 gallons oil capacity and 6 gallons air space, one in each engine nacelle.

   (ii) There are no separate oil cooler controls.

   (iii) An oil dilution system is fitted and is controlled by pushbuttons mounted in the engine nacelles.

MAIN SERVICES

7. **Hydraulic system**

   (i) Two engine-driven pumps, one on each engine, supply hydraulic pressure for operation of the

   > Flaps
   > Undercarriage

   The system will function on one pump, but at a reduced rate.

   (ii) On the ground, and whenever the normal system is in use, the white topped hydraulic power lever (1), fitted outboard of the flaps position indicator, must be ON.

PART I—DESCRIPTIVE

(iii) In the air the hydraulic power lever must be moved forward to the OFF position; this operates a by-pass valve and prevents the engine-driven pumps from overheating and consequent failure.

(iv) A handpump (21) is mounted outboard of the elevator trimming tab control, for use if engine-driven pump pressure is not available.

(v) In the event of failure of the normal system the flaps and undercarriage may be lowered through an emergency system which employs separate pipe lines. This system is brought into operation by an emergency selector lever (2) which is mounted outboard of the normal hydraulic power lever and with which it is interconnected (*see* para. 68).

8. Pneumatic system

A compressor on the starboard engine charges a bottle for the operation of the

>   Brakes
>   Fuel jettison valves
>   Guns
>   Landing flare release (if fitted)

The available pressure is shown on a triple reading gauge mounted on the bottom left-hand side of the instrument panel.

Normal operating pressure is 220 lb./sq. in.

9. Electrical system

(i) A generator on the starboard engine, and a 24-volt battery, supply power for the operation of the whole of the electrical system.

(ii) An 80-volt alternator on the port engine supplies current for the special radar equipment when this is fitted.

(iii) A generator warning light is mounted on the rear face of the main fuze panel, which is fitted on the port side of the fuselage above the ammunition boxes. The light will come on whenever the generator is not delivering

PART I—DESCRIPTIVE

current. On the ground, when the starboard engine is not running, the light will remain on unless the battery is disconnected. The current consumed, however, is negligible.

(iv) A ground starter battery socket is fitted on the starboard side of the fuselage, just forward of the front entrance hatch.

AIRCRAFT CONTROLS

10. Flying controls

The pendulum type rudder pedals are adjustable for reach during flight by means of the crank handle at the bottom centre of the instrument panel.

11. Flying controls locking gear

Three tubular rods which are pivoted together are used to lock the flying controls. The clip between the two longer rods is attached to the left-hand side of the aileron control handwheel and a fork ended pin at the other joint passes through a hollow bolt at the base of the control column. The end of the short rod is clipped on to the left rudder pedal while the long rod is fastened by a pin to a short strut on the left-hand cockpit shelf. When not in use the locking gear is stowed in the roof above the pilot's entrance hatch.

12. Trimming tab controls

The elevator trimming tab control handwheel (19) is on the right of the cockpit level with the pilot's knee. The tab angle indicator (22) is outboard of the handwheel and below it.

The rudder trimming tab control (18) and indicator are on the right-hand cockpit shelf. The aileron trimming tab (56) control and indicator are on the rear face of the right-hand cockpit shelf. All these controls work in the natural sense.

PART I—DESCRIPTIVE

13. **Undercarriage**

   (i) The undercarriage can be raised by two methods and lowered by three :

UP or DOWN by the normal system. Hydraulic power lever ON. Emergency selector lever OFF.	Supply through the normal system.	With pressure provided by the engine-driven pumps.
UP or DOWN by the normal system. Hydraulic power lever ON. Emergency selector lever OFF.	Supply through the normal system.	With pressure provided by the handpump if engine-driven pump pressure is not available.
DOWN only by the emergency system. Hydraulic power lever OFF. Emergency selector lever ON.	Supply through the emergency system.	

   (ii) The undercarriage selector lever (26), marked UP—UNDERCARRIAGE—DOWN, incorporates a spring-loaded pin which locks the lever in the down position when the aircraft is on the ground.

   (iii) The emergency selector lever (2), marked ON—EMERGENCY—OFF, which is mounted outboard of the hydraulic power lever, has a safety guard which prevents it being set to ON unless the hydraulic power lever is in the OFF (forward) position.

   > NOTE.—The emergency selector lever must be returned to the OFF position before the hydraulic power lever can be moved to ON.

PART I—DESCRIPTIVE

(iv) When the aircraft is on the ground, safety locking pins should be inserted in the knuckle joints on the inboard radius rods of each undercarriage unit.

Before take-off the pins must be removed and stowed in a bag in the observer's compartment.

14. Undercarriage position indicators

The undercarriage position indicators (4) are on the bottom left-hand side of the instrument panel and are switched on and off by the electrical services switch (24). Indications are :

Main wheels and tail wheel locked down—
    DOWN on green background.

Main wheels and tail wheel locked up—
    UP on red background.

Wheels between locks—   Black and white dazzle lines.

NOTE.— (i) A warning horn sounds if the throttles are less than one-third open when any wheel is not locked down.

(ii) Whenever the indicators are suspect, or at night, the handpump should be checked for " solidity " thus ensuring that the undercarriage is locked correctly. If high resistance does not build up immediately, or even if felt, should the indicator not show DOWN do not continue pumping through the main lines, but set the emergency selector ON (power lever OFF) and then pump—*see* para. 68.

15. Flaps control

The flaps are controlled by a black topped lever (27) marked UP—FLAPS—DOWN, which is fitted outboard of the undercarriage selector lever. The lever should be returned to the neutral (mid) position after any operation. Intermediate settings may be obtained by returning the lever to the neutral position when the desired flap angle is reached.

PART I—DESCRIPTIVE

16. **Flaps position indicator**

    The setting of the flaps is shown on the indicator outboard of the flap control lever. The indicator is connected to the flaps by a flexible cable and is calibrated throughout the flaps range. A thick white line at 20° indicates the maximum lift setting.

17. **Wheel brakes**

    The brake control lever (14) and parking catch are mounted on the aileron control handwheel. Differential braking is afforded by means of a relay valve connected to the rudder pedals.

ENGINE CONTROLS

18. **Throttle controls**

    The friction control knob for the throttle levers (37) is on the inboard side of the engine controls box. The throttle quadrants are gated at the CRUISING and RATED positions.

19. **Mixture controls**

    Mixture control is entirely automatic, being governed by the setting of the throttle levers.

    An economical mixture strength is obtained only when these are at or behind the CRUISING gates.

    Note.—Throttle settings between the CRUISING and RATED gates promote unsuitable mixture strengths and must not, therefore, be used continuously.

20. **Propeller controls**

    (i) The speed control levers (36) for the hydromatic propellers, which vary the governed r.p.m. from 2,900 to 1,600, are mounted together in a quadrant outboard of the throttle quadrants. A friction control knob is fitted.

    (ii) The feathering pushbuttons (6) are mounted together on the top left-hand side of the instrument panel.

PART I—DESCRIPTIVE

21. **Supercharger controls**

    The two-speed supercharger control (41), marked " M " RATIO—TWO SPEED BLOWER—" S " RATIO, are mounted on the left-hand shelf aft of the engine controls box. Hercules XVII engines have superchargers locked in " M " low gear.

    NOTE.—When changing gear the controls must always be moved smartly and without pause.

22. **Cowling gills controls**

    The two cowling gill motor switches (42) are mounted aft of the supercharger controls. They have three positions, OPEN, OFF and CLOSED. The knobs must be depressed when setting the switches to OPEN or CLOSED. When the required setting is obtained the switches should be returned to the OFF position and the knobs then pulled out.

    Red warning lights fitted next to the switches indicate when the motors are running. No gills position indicator is fitted, but their position can be observed from the cockpit.

23. **Carburettor air-intake heat controls**

    The two levers (35) mounted in a quadrant outboard of the supercharger controls are moved forward for COLD AIR and back for HOT AIR.

24. **Ignition switches**

    These are mounted on the bottom centre of the instrument panel. They cannot be moved to the ON position until the electrical services switch is ON.

25. **Engine starting controls**

    The shielded engine starter and booster-coil pushbuttons are mounted on the right-hand side of the instrument panel outboard of the engine speed indicators.

26. **Slow-running cut-out controls**

    The two spring-loaded knobs (29), marked ENGINE CUT-OUTS, which are fitted on the left-hand side of the cockpit aft of the pilot's seat, are pulled out and held to stop the engines.

PART I—DESCRIPTIVE

OPERATIONAL CONTROLS

27. **Torpedo sight**

    A manually operated sighting control (8) is mounted on the left-hand side of the instrument panel below the oil pressure gauges. The torpedo sight ON—OFF (13) and dimmer switches are mounted on the framing of the right-hand side panel of the windscreen.

28. **Torpedo depth setting control**

    The control handle with integral depth indicator is under a hinged cover on the floor forward of the observer's seat.

29. **Torpedo and bomb master selector switches**

    These are mounted on the right-hand window sill. A red warning light comes on when the desired store has been selected and goes out after release. If the store fails to release the light will remain on. A shielded jettison pushbutton is mounted aft of the selector switches.

30. **Bomb fusing switches**

    These are fitted on a small panel below the master selector switches.

31. **Torpedo and bomb firing pushbutton**

    The pushbutton (38) incorporated in the top of the starboard throttle lever releases the torpedo or bombs and automatically operates the torpedo camera if this has been preselected by the switch on the right-hand cockpit wall.

32. **R/P switches**

    (i) The R/P master switch is mounted on the left-hand cockpit wall below the V.H.F. radio controller.

    (ii) The R/P selector switch (7) is mounted below the left-hand corner of the windscreen and is marked PAIRS—R.P. SELECTOR—SALVO.

33. **R/P Firing pushbutton**

    This is mounted on the aileron control hand wheel next to the gun firing pushbutton.

PART I—DESCRIPTIVE

34. **R/P rails jettison control**

    This is mounted on the right-hand cockpit wall. It is painted red and is secured by a strap in the safe position.

35. **Gun sight**

    A reflector gun sight (12) is fitted above the instrument panel on a swivelling arm which permits it to be swung clear of the windscreen when not in use. A dimmer switch for the gun sight is mounted on the top left-hand side of the instrument panel below the R/P selector switch.

36. **Gun firing pushbutton**

    The selective firing pushbutton on the aileron control handwheel is fitted with a spring loaded safety flap. When the flap is at SAFE the camera gun can be fired by pressing the projection on the inboard side of the pushbutton. When it is set to FIRE the pushbutton will fire the cannon and operate the camera gun simultaneously.

OTHER CONTROLS

37. **Cockpit heating and ventilating controls**
    (i) The supply of heated air is controlled by a two-position lever on the left-hand cockpit wall level with the pilot's shoulder.
    (ii) A ventilator is mounted on the right-hand side of the instrument panel above the engine starter and booster-coil pushbutton.

38. **Cockpit lighting**
    (i) A swivelling floodlight is mounted on the framing of each side panel of the windscreen.
    The dimmer switches for these lights are on either side of the instrument panel, one above the undercarriage position indicators and the other above the ventilator.
    (ii) Two U/V floodlights and an emergency floodlight are mounted on the control column.
    The U/V lights are controlled by a rheostat on the right-hand cockpit wall above the aileron trimming tab control, and the emergency light is switched on and off by the switch just forward of this rheostat.

PART I—DESCRIPTIVE

39. **Pilot's seat collapsing lever**

    In order to facilitate escape from the cockpit the pilot's seat can be tilted backwards by pulling up the lever (45) on the right-hand side of the seat.

    NOTE.— (i) Before the lever can be moved the knob in the top of the lever must be depressed.

    (ii) Before take-off care must be taken to ensure that the lever is in the down position and that the seat is correctly locked and cannot collapse.

40. **Windscreen wiper and de-icing controls**

    (i) The windscreen wiper is controlled by a rheostat mounted on a bracket on the right-hand side of the instrument panel. Just above the rheostat there is an isolating switch which ensures that battery power is not wasted by leaving the rheostat slightly on when the wiper is not in use.

    NOTE.—The wiper should not be used when the windscreen is dry.

    (ii) A windscreen de-icing pump (20) and flow control is mounted on the right-hand cockpit shelf immediately aft of the rudder trimming tab control.

41. **R.I. Compass**

    The R.I. compass, which is mounted on a bracket on the right-hand side of the instrument panel, is controlled by a two-position switch on the right-hand cockpit wall above the aileron trimming tab control.

A.P. 1721H—P.N.
Pilot's Notes

PART II
HANDLING

NOTE.—All speeds quoted apply when the Pilot's A.S.I. is connected to the pitot and static sides of the pressure head mounted beneath the port wing.

42. Management of the fuel system

(i) Start the engines, warm up, taxy, take-off and climb on the inner tanks, then change to the outer tanks and use them until they are exhausted.

NOTE.—If flying very low the inner tanks should be re-selected when the outer tanks each contain 20 gallons of fuel.

(ii) The SUCTION BALANCE cock should be kept OFF unless

(*a*) all fuel on one side has been lost or consumed;
(*b*) an engine has failed (*see* para. 64).

(iii) When a drop tank is carried

(*a*) take off on the inner tanks and continue to fly on these tanks for 45 minutes, then turn ON the drop tank cock.
(*b*) when the air pressure gauge reads less than 2 lb./sq. in. the drop tank cock should be turned OFF.

43. Preliminaries

(i) On entering the cockpit check:

Ignition switches ...	OFF
Hydraulic power lever ...	ON
Undercarriage selector lever	DOWN, lever locking pin engaged.
Pneumatic supply pressure	Normally 220 lb./sq. in.

then switch on the electrical services switch and check:

Undercarriage position indicators	DOWN.
Fuel contents gauges	

(ii) Check the flying controls for full and free movement.

PART II—HANDLING

44. Starting the engines and warming up

(i) Set the controls as follows:

Fuel cocks	INNER TANK ON.
	Suction balance cock OFF.
	Drop tank cock OFF.
Throttles	¾-inch open
Propeller speed control levers	Fully forward
Supercharger controls	M RATIO (low gear)
Carburettor air intake heat controls	COLD.
Cowling gills	OPEN

(ii) Have each engine turned by hand through at least two revolutions of the propeller to ensure that there is no possibility of hydraulic shock damage.

(iii) Instruct the ground crew to operate the Ki-gass priming pumps until the suction and delivery pipelines are full (this may be judged by a sudden increase in resistance), then have the engines primed with the following number of strokes if they are cold: if K.40 (40 c.c. effective) pumps are fitted, divide by four, giving an incomplete stroke where necessary.

Air temp. °C.	+30	+20	+10	0	−10	−20
Normal fuel	3	4	7	12	—	—
High volatility fuel	—	—	—	4	8	18

NOTE.—High volatility fuel should be used at air temperatures below freezing.

(iv) have a ground starter battery plugged in, then switch on the ignition and press the starter and booster-coil pushbuttons. Turning periods must not exceed 20 seconds with 30-second intervals between each period.

(v) The engine should start immediately, but it may be necessary for the ground crew to continue priming until it picks up and runs smoothly on the carburettor.

(vi) When both engines are running satisfactorily have the Ki-gass priming pumps screwed down and the ground starter battery disconnected.

PART II—HANDLING

(vii) Run the engines at their lowest steady speed for about one minute, then open up gradually to 1,000 r.p.m. and warm up at this speed.

> NOTE.—In very cold weather the engines should be run at their lowest steady speed for 3-4 minutes to avoid the possibility of damaging the oil coolers.

45. Testing the engines and services

While warming up :

(i) Check all temperatures and pressures and test the operation of the hydraulic system by lowering and raising the flaps.

(ii) Test each magneto as a precautionary check before increasing power further.

(iii) Check the functioning of both vacuum pumps by operating the changeover cock which is mounted on the bottom left-hand side of the instrument panel.

After warming up to 120° C. (cylinder) and 15° C. (oil) :
For each engine in turn :

(iv) Open the throttle to give 0 lb./sq. in. boost and check that all cylinders are operating by verifying that r.p.m. are within 50 of those normally obtained.

> NOTE.—While the starboard engine is running at this power setting, the observer should check that the generator is charging the battery.

(v) On aircraft which have Hercules XVIII engines throttle back until r.p.m. fall to 2,400, then check :

(a) The operation of the supercharger gear change by changing to S RATIO (high gear), noting the momentary drop in oil pressure and the flicker of the E.S.I.

(b) The correct engagement of the S RATIO (high gear) clutches by noting that boost is maintained after the change to high gear is made and that r.p.m. drop to 2,300-2,320 when running in that gear. Then, after 30 seconds, change back to M RATIO (low gear).

(vi) Exercise and check the operation of the constant-speed propeller by moving the speed control lever over its full governing range at least twice. Return the speed control lever fully forward.

(vii) Test each magneto in turn. If the engine is running smoothly but the single ignition drop exceeds 50 r.p.m. the ignition should be checked at higher power (*see* sub. para. (ix) below). If there is marked vibration the engine should be stopped and the fault investigated.

> NOTE.—The following additional comprehensive checks should be carried out after repair, inspection, other than daily, or at any time at the discretion of the pilot.

(viii) Open the throttle fully and check boost and static r.p.m.

> NOTE.—+10 lb./sq. in. boost will not be obtained without " ram " (see para. 57 (iii)).

(ix) Throttle back to the RATED gate, or further if necessary to ensure that r.p.m. fall below the take-off figure (2,900) and test each magneto in turn. If the single-ignition drop exceeds 50 r.p.m. the aircraft should not be flown.

46. Taxying

Before taxying check :

(i) that the ground crew remove and hold up the undercarriage safety locking pins and that they hand them to the observer for stowage.

(ii) that all the entrance hatches are closed and fastened securely.

(iii) the brake pressure and pneumatic supply pressure. Normally the latter should be 220 lb./sq. in. If it is lower check that it has built up while warming up and testing the starboard engine.

PART II—HANDLING

47. Check list before take-off

H—Hydraulic
   power lever ... ON.

T—Trimming Tabs

Elevator ...	At full load (including torpedo)	At normal full load (no torpedo, drop tank, or other external stores).
	"TAKE-OFF" on indicator.	$\frac{1}{8}$-inch aft of "TAKE-OFF" on indicator.

Rudder ... ⎫
Aileron ... ⎬ Neutral.

P—Propeller
   speed control
   levers   ... Fully forward.

F—Fuel   ... Cocks to INNER TANK ON.
               Suction balance cock OFF.
               Drop tank cock OFF.

F—Flaps ... Up at light load, 15° down at heavy load, selector neutral.

Cowling gills $\frac{1}{3}$ open.

Superchargers Low gear.

Carburettor air-
   intake heat
   controls ... COLD.

NOTE.—When a torpedo is carried the master selector switch should be set to ON before take-off, so that in an emergency it can be jettisoned immediately.

48. Take-off

(i) Align the aircraft carefully on the runway making certain that the tailwheel is straight.

(ii) Check by opening up against the brakes that both engines are responding evenly, then throttle back, release the

PART II—HANDLING

brakes and open the throttles slowly and evenly, keeping straight by coarse use of the rudder.

> NOTE.—Between the CRUISING and RATED gates power increases rapidly for only a small increase in throttle opening. It is, therefore, important to ease both throttles through the CRUISING gates simultaneously; if this is not done a swing may easily be induced.

(iii) Raise the tail early in the take-off run to improve rudder control.

(iv) Safety speed at full load (including torpedo) at full take-off power, flaps up or 15° down, is 170 knots (198 m.p.h.) I.A.S.

(v) Raise the flaps (if used) at 300 ft. then set the hydraulic power lever to OFF.

(vi) If a torpedo is carried return the master selector switch to OFF at 1,000 ft.

49. Climbing

The recommended climbing speed is 150 knots (172 m.p.h.) I.A.S.

50. General flying

(i) *Stability*

At all normal loads stability about all axes is satisfactory.

(ii) *Changes of trim*

Undercarriage up	... Nose up.
Undercarriage down	Nose down.
Flaps up ...	... Nose down (the change of trim over the last 20° of flap movement is marked).
Flaps down ...	... Nose up (the change of trim over the first 20° of flap movement is marked).
Cowling gills open	... Nose down.
Cowling gills closed	... Nose up.

PART II—HANDLING

(iii) *Controls*

The elevator and elevator trimming tab controls are light and powerful and must be used with care.

(iv) *Supercharger exercising*

On aircraft which have Hercules XVIII engines every endeavour should be made to change to high gear once every 2 hours during the course of a long flight to avoid the possibility of sludging of the clutch plates.

NOTE.—Supercharger gear changes should not be made at power in excess of 0 lb./sq. in. boost, 2,400 r.p.m.

(v) *Propellers*

With " paddle bladed " propellers there is a tendency to engine overspeeding when power is increased rapidly or during dives. The propeller speed control levers must always be moved slowly and carefully and rapid throttle opening must be avoided.

(vi) *Flying at reduced airspeed in conditions of poor visibility*

Reduce speed to 150 knots (172 m.p.h.) I.A.S. and lower the flaps 20°. Set the propeller speed control levers to give 2,400 r.p.m. Speed may then be reduced to 130 knots (150 m.p.h.) I.A.S.

(vii) *P4 compass inaccuracy*

Firing the cannon is likely to alter the deviation of the P4 compass considerably. Both the R.I. compass and the Observer's compass, however, remain unaffected.

51. Stalling

(i) The stalling speeds, engines " off," in knots (m.p.h.) I.A.S. are:

	At full load (including torpedo)	At full normal load (no torpedo drop tank or other external stores)
Flaps and undercarriage up ...	96 (110)	90 (104)
Flaps and undercarriage down	75 (86)	70 (80)

PART II—HANDLING

(ii) With the flaps and undercarriage up some warning of the approach of a stall is given by elevator buffeting the onset of which can be felt some 10-12 knots (12-14 m.p.h.) I.A.S. before the stall itself. Just before the stall the right wing tends to drop. This tendency can be checked by use of the ailerons: the nose then drops gently.

(iii) With the flaps and undercarriage down warning of the approach of a stall is less pronounced. At the stall the right wing drops sharply.

(iv) In all cases the recovery from a stall is straightforward and easy.

52. Diving

The aircraft becomes increasingly tail heavy as speed is gained and should therefore be trimmed into and during the dive.

53. Approach and landing

(i) On entering the circuit check:

Pneumatic supply pressure	220 lb./sq. in.
Cowling gills	CLOSED.
Superchargers	Low gear.
Carburettor air intake heat controls	COLD.

Then reduce speed to 150 knots (172 m.p.h.) I.A.S. and check:

H —Hydraulic power lever	ON.
U —Undercarriage ...	DOWN, check by indicators and warning horn.
P —Propeller speed control levers	Set for 2,400 r.p.m.
F —Fuel	Fullest tanks.
F —Flaps	20° down; fully down after the final turn into wind.

PART II—HANDLING

(ii) The recommended final approach speeds in knots (m.p.h.) I.A.S. are:

	At all loads up to the maximum permissible for landing (22,100 lb.)	
	Flaps down	*Flaps up.*
Engine assisted ...	100 (115)	105 (120)
Glide	110 (126)	—

The initial straight approach should, however, be made at a speed some 15 knots (18 m.p.h.) I.A.S. above these figures.

NOTE.—If a landing is to be made with a torpedo slung the speeds quoted above should be increased by at least 5 knots (6 m.p.h.) I.A.S.

54. Mislanding

(i) With the flaps and undercarriage down the aircraft will climb away easily at climbing power.

(ii) Raise the undercarriage immediately.

(iii) With the flaps fully down climb at 105 knots (120 m.p.h.) I.A.S.

(iv) As soon as the undercarriage is up raise the flaps to 20° down and increase speed to 120 knots (140 m.p.h.) I.A.S.

(v) At 300 ft. raise the flaps fully and retrim.

PART II—HANDLING

55. Beam approach

AIRCRAFT TYPE.—BEAUFIGHTER T.F. Mk. X. Return of sortie loading. No ammunition, half fuel remaining (i.e. about 19,500 lb.).

	Preliminary Approach	At Inner Marker on Q.D.R.	At Outer Marker on Q.D.R.	At Outer Marker on Q.D.M.	At Inner Marker on Q.D.M.
Indicated height (feet)	1,500	1,500	1,000	800	100
Action	Set the cowling gills ½ open. Lower the flaps 20°.*	—	Lower the undercarriage.	Lower the flaps fully.	Throttle back slowly.
Resultant change of trim	Strongly nose up.	—	Slightly nose down	—	—
I.A.S.	140 knots (160 m.p.h.)	140 knots (160 m.p.h.)	120 knots (140 m.p.h.)	105 knots (120 m.p.h.)	95 knots (110 m.p.h.)
R.P.M.	2,400	2,400	2,400	2,400	2,400
Boost (level flight)	−4 lb./sq. in.	−4 lb./sq. in.	−1 lb./sq. in.	0 lb./sq. in.	—
Boost (−500 ft./min.)	−6 lb./sq. in.	−6 lb./sq. in.	−3½ lb./sq. in.	−2 lb./sq. in.	—
Boost (overshoot)	—	—	—	—	+6 lb./sq. in.

Remarks—*see paragraph 59 (ii)	OVERSHOOT
Altimeter error at take-off −50 feet. Altimeter at touch down −40 feet. Add 1 millibar to Q.F.E. to give zero reading at touchdown.	Open the throttles evenly to the RATED gates. Raise the undercarriage. Climb at 105 knots (120 m.p.h.) I.A.S. and raise the flaps in one movement at 300 ft., retrimming as required.

PART II—HANDLING

56. After landing

(i) Before taxying raise the flaps and open the cowling gills

On reaching dispersal :

(ii) On aircraft which have Hercules XVIII engines exercise the superchargers once (*see* para. 45 (v)). On aircraft with Hercules XVII engines open the throttles smoothly and slowly to give -2 lb./sq. in. boost, then on all aircraft.

(iii) Close the throttles slowly until r.p.m. fall to 800-900 and run at this speed for 2 minutes.

(iv) Stop the engines by pulling out the slow running cut-out controls.

(v) Should a back-fire occur at any stage, open up to -2 lb./sq. in. and repeat the above procedure.

(vi) When the engines have stopped turn off the fuel, switch off the ignition, and when the engines have cooled close the cowling gills, then switch off all other electrical services.

(vii) *Oil Dilution* (*see* A.P. 2095).

The correct dilution period for these engines is 1 minute.

(viii) On leaving the cockpit ensure that the undercarriage safety locking pins are inserted in the knuckle joints of each undercarriage unit.

A.P. 1721H—P.N.
Pilot's Notes

PART III

OPERATING DATA

57. Engine data—Hercules XVII and XVIII

(i) Fuel—100/130 grade.

(ii) Oil—*see* A.P. 1464/C37.

(iii) The principal engine limitations are as follows:

	Super-charger gear†	R.P.M.	Boost lb./sq. in.	Temp. °C. Cyl.	Temp. °C. Oil
MAX. TAKE-OFF TO 1,000 FT. ...	M	2,900	+10*	230 at start of take-off	—
MAX. CLIMBING 1 HOUR LIMIT	M } S	2,400	+6	290	90
MAX. RICH CONTINUOUS ...	M } S	2,400	+6	290	80
MAX. WEAK CONTINUOUS ...	M } S	2,400	+2	290	80
COMBAT 5 MINS. LIMIT ...	M } S	2,900	+10*	300	100

† S (high) gear is not operative on Hercules XVII engines.

* With the "ram" effect obtainable in level flight, boost should be +10 lb./sq. in. at low altitude.

With the aircraft stationary boost will probably not exceed +8¼ lb./sq. in.

OIL PRESSURE: NORMAL ... ... 80–90 lb./sq. in.
                EMERGENCY MINIMUM
                  (5 MINS.) ... ... 60 lb./sq. in.

MINM. TEMP. FOR TAKE-OFF—
    OIL: NORMAL ... ... 15° C.
        OPERATIONAL NECESSITY ... ... 5° C.
    CYL: ... ... 120° C.
MAX. TEMP. FOR STOPPING ENGINE—CYL. ... 230° C.

PART III—OPERATING DATA

58. Position error corrections

At 23,000 lb. the corrections for position error are:

FROM	100	120	140	160	180	200	220	240	260	280	m.p.h.
TO	120	140	160	180	200	220	240	260	280	300	m.p.h.
ADD	7	5	3	1	—	—	—	—	—	—	knots or m.p.h.
SUBTRACT	—	—	—	—	1	2	4	6	7	8	
FROM	87	104	121	139	156	174	190	208	226	243	knots
TO	104	121	139	156	174	190	208	226	243	260	knots

59. Flying limitations

(i) The aircraft is designed for the duties of a long-range reconnaissance fighter. Intentional spinning and aerobatics are prohibited.

(ii) *Maximum speeds in knots (m.p.h.) I.A.S.*

Diving :

(*a*) Without external stores 345 (400)

(*b*) With 8 × 60 lb. R/P 300 (345)

(*c*) With torpedo 320 (370)

NOTE.—When carrying 2 × 500 lb. bombs and 2 × 250 lb. depth charges, it is recommended that a speed of 325 knots (375 m.p.h.) should not be exceeded and with 8 × 60 lb. R.P. a speed of 300 knots (345 m.p.h.) should not be exceeded.

Lowering flaps 175 (200)

Flaps fully down 116 (135)

Lowering undercarriage 150 (170)

Undercarriage down 130 (150)

Jettisoning drop tank 210 (240)

PART III—OPERATING DATA

(iii) *Maximum weights*

For take-off and gentle manoeuvres ... 25,500 lb.†
For all forms of flying ... ... 22,100 lb.
For landing ... ... 22,100 lb.*

† For training the take-off weight should not exceed 21,000 lb.

* In emergency the aircraft may be landed on prepared runways at weights up to 25,000 lb. provided that
  (a) Mod. T.402 is incorporated.
  (b) AIR 32160.1 type main undercarriage units are fitted.

60. Maximum performance

(i) *Climbing*

(a) The speed for maximum rate of climb is 130 knots (150 m.p.h.) I.A.S. from sea level to 12,000 ft., thereafter reducing speed by 1 knot or m.p.h. I.A.S. per 1,000 ft.

Since this speed is less than safety speed at climbing power it is recommended that an initial climbing speed of 150 knots (172 m.p.h.) I.A.S. should be maintained at least until the boost in low gear falls and further if the maximum rate of climb is not essential.

(b) On aircraft which have Hercules XVIII engines change to high gear when the boost in low gear has fallen to +4 lb./sq. in.

NOTE.—Throttle back to 0 lb./sq. in. boost before engaging high gear, then set the throttles to the RATED gates again.

(ii) *Combat*

(a) Set the propeller speed control levers fully forward and open the throttles fully. If the maximum obtainable boost is +7 lb./sq. in. or less, throttle back to the RATED gates.

(b) On aircraft which have Hercules XVIII engines change to high gear if the maximum obtainable boost in low gear is +7 lb./sq. in.

NOTE.—If possible power should be reduced to 0 lb./sq. in. boost, 2,400 r.p.m., before the change to high gear is made (*see* para. 50 (iv)).

PART III—OPERATING DATA

61. Maximum range (*see* Curves, page 35)

(i) *Climbing*

Set the propeller speed control levers to give 2,400 r.p.m., the throttles to the RATED gates and climb at 150 knots (172 m.p.h.) I.A.S. Change to high gear when the boost in low gear has fallen to +4 lb./sq. in.

NOTE.—Throttle back to 0 lb./sq. in. boost before engaging high gear, then set the throttles to the RATED gates again.

(ii) *Cruising*

(*a*) The recommended speed for maximum range is 175 knots (200 m.p.h.) I.A.S.

(*b*) Set the throttles to the CRUISING gates and obtain the recommended speed by adjusting r.p.m. between 2,400 and 1,600.

NOTE.—R.p.m. which promote rough running must be avoided at all times.

(*c*) At moderate and high altitudes change to high gear if the recommended speed cannot be maintained with the throttles at the CRUISING gates and the propeller speed control lever set to give 2,400 r.p.m.

62. Fuel capacities and consumptions

(i) *Fuel capacities*

MAIN SUPPLY	Permanent tanks galls.	Aux. tanks galls.	Max. capacity galls.
Inner wing tanks (2 × 188)	376	—	—
Outer wing tanks (2 × 87)	174		550
LONG RANGE WING TANKS (24 + 29 + 29 + 50)	132		132
FUSELAGE DROP TANK (1 × 200) ...		200	200
Totals	682	200	882

PART III—OPERATING DATA

(ii) *Fuel consumptions*

(*a*) The approximate total fuel consumption in the rich mixture range is

Boost lb./sq. in.	R.P.M.	Gallons/hour
+10	2,900	400
+ 8¼	2,900	376
+ 6	2,900	346
	2,400	254

(*b*) The approximate total fuel consumption (gallons/hour) in the weak mixture range is,

(i) Low gear at 2,000 ft.

Boost lb./sq. in.	R.p.m.					
	2,400	2,200	2,000	1,800	1,700	1,600
+2	125	115	106	96	91	—
+1	115	108	100	91	86	82
0	109	101	94	86	81	77
−1	104	95	86	77	73	69
−2			81	72	68	64
−3				67	64	60
−4				63	60	57

NOTE.—For every 1,000 ft. above or below this height add or subtract ½ gallon per hour.

(ii) High gear at 10,000 ft.

Boost lb./sq. in.	R.p.m.					
	2,400	2,200	2,000	1,800	1,700	1,600
+2	123	116	108			
+1	118	110	103			
0	110	102	95	89	84	
−1	102	95	89	82	79	75
−2	96	89	83	76	73	69
−3	88	81	75	69	66	63
−4	81	76	71	65	62	58

NOTE.—For every 1,000 ft. above or below this height add or subtract 1 gallon per hour.

PART III—OPERATING DATA

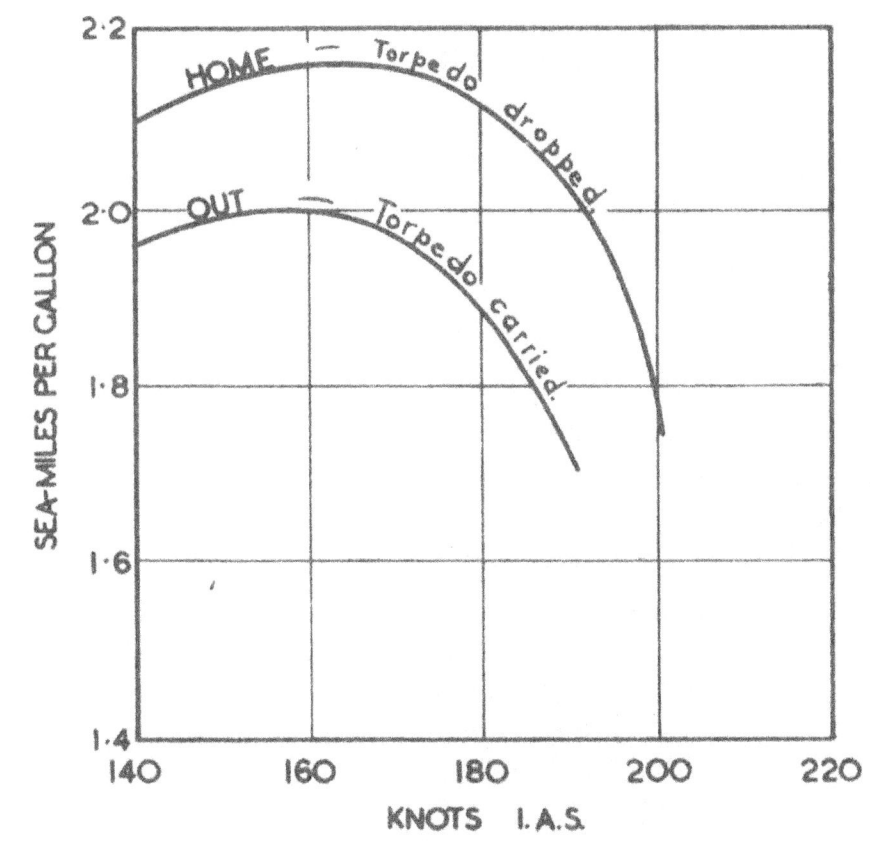

A.P. 1721H—P.N.
Pilot's Notes

PART IV
EMERGENCIES

63. Engine failure after take-off

(i) Safety speed at full load (including torpedo), at full take-off power, flaps up or 15° down, is 170 knots (196 m.p.h.) I.A.S.

(ii) If safety speed has been attained the aircraft will climb away comfortably on either engine at climbing power at about 150 knots (172 m.p.h.) I.A.S., provided that,

(*a*) the torpedo is jettisoned;

(*b*) the propeller of the failed engine is feathered and the gills are closed on that side;

(*c*) the flaps are fully up.

NOTE.—The drag of a windmilling " paddle-bladed " propeller is very high and unless feathering action is taken immediately an engine fails control can only be retained at the expense of a rapid loss of height.

64. Engine failure in flight

(i) Close the throttle of the failed engine and feather its propeller (*see* para. 65).

NOTE.—The windmilling drag of a " paddle-bladed " propeller is very high and unless feathering action is taken immediately an engine fails control difficulties may be experienced, especially if the failure occurs on a high power climb. Under these circumstances it will generally be necessary to throttle back the live engine to prevent control being lost.

(ii) In order to use the fuel from the tanks on the failed engine side

(*a*) set the SUCTION BALANCE cock ON;

(*b*) turn OFF the main tanks cock on the live engine side.

PART IV—EMERGENCIES

(iii) When the tanks on the failed engine side each contain 20 gallons of fuel,
  (a) set the main tanks cock on the live engine side to the fuller tank ;
  (b) set the SUCTION BALANCE cock OFF ;
  (c) turn OFF the main tanks cock on the failed engine side.
(iv) At full load in favourable conditions height can be maintained on either engine at full climbing power at 145-150 knots (167-172 m.p.h.) I.A.S.
(v) In single-engine flight the rudder must be used with great care. It is a powerful and sensitive control and if used coarsely can promote considerable yaw and roll.

65. Feathering
(i) Close the throttle immediately.
(ii) Hold the feathering pushbutton in only long enough to ensure that it stays in by itself, then release it so that it can spring out when feathering is complete.
(iii) Switch off the ignition when the propeller has stopped, or nearly stopped, rotating, then close the gills.
  NOTE.—Should engine failure occur early after take-off (ii) may precede (i).

66. Unfeathering
(i) Set the propeller speed control lever fully back and ensure that the throttle is closed.
(ii) Switch on the ignition and press the feathering pushbutton, releasing it when r.p.m. rise to 800-1,000.
  NOTE.—(a) If the propeller does not return to normal constant-speed operation it must be re-feathered and unfeathered again, the feathering pushbutton then being released at slightly higher r.p.m.
  (b) To avoid the risk of engine overspeeding a propeller should not be unfeathered at speeds above normal cruising speed.
  (c) There is a generator only on the starboard engine. When the propeller of this engine is feathered, therefore, it is important to switch off all non-essential electrical services.

PART IV—EMERGENCIES

67. Fuel jettisoning

(i) The fuel in the wing tanks, except that contained in No. 1 L.R. tanks, can be jettisoned by operating the PORT and STBD. JETTISON RELEASE levers (25), which are mounted on the bottom left-hand side of the instrument panel above the electrical services switch.

(ii) When all the tanks are full the main bulk of the fuel can be jettisoned in about one minute.

(iii) When it is desired to jettison only a part of the fuel load the levers should be operated for a few seconds at a time. The fuel contents gauges should then be checked after each operation.

> NOTE.—If the pneumatic supply pressure is below 80 lb. sq. in. the fuel jettison valves cannot be operated.

68. Undercarriage and flaps emergency operation

(i) Should the undercarriage or flaps fail to lower when selected normally, set the emergency selector lever to ON (this automatically moves the hydraulic power lever to OFF and, the flap lever from UP to NEUTRAL): operate the handpump.

> NOTE.—(a) If the undercarriage up locks fail to release, very considerable pressure may be required on the handpump to free them.
>
> (b) With the flap lever at NEUTRAL the undercarriage will come down without the flaps: to lower the flaps the flap lever must be at DOWN.
>
> (c) The undercarriage and flaps cannot be raised through the emergency system.

(ii) If the emergency system fails, set the emergency lever OFF and the power lever ON, then try the handpump through the normal system.

69. Single-engine landing

(i) A left-hand circuit can safely be made (and is recommended) irrespective of which engine has failed.

(ii) While manoeuvring with the undercarriage and flaps up, maintain a speed of at least 140 knots (160 m.p.h.) I.A.S.

PART IV—EMERGENCIES

(iii) Keep extra height in hand if possible and lower the undercarriage as late as practicable, aiming to have it locked down just before the final straight approach.

(iv) When cross wind preparatory to turning into the airfield the flaps may then be lowered 20°. They should not be lowered further until it is clear that the landing area is within easy reach.

(v) The live engine should be used carefully to regulate the rate of descent throughout the approach, the final stage of which should be made at a speed of 95-100 knots (110-115 m.p.h.) I.A.S.

70. **Fire-extinguishers**

(i) Two shielded pushbuttons (9) on the top left-hand side of the instrument panel, behind the propeller feathering pushbuttons, operate the engine fire-extinguishers (in the event of a crash operation is automatic).

(ii) There are two engine fire warning lights on the top right-hand side of the instrument panel.

(iii) Two hand fire-extinguishers are stowed at convenient points within the fuselage.

71. **Torpedo, bomb, R/P rails and drop tank jettisoning**

(i) The torpedo or bombs can be jettisoned when the master selector switches (15) are ON by pressing the shielded pushbutton (46) on the switch panel on the right-hand window sill.

(ii) The R/P rails can be jettisoned by pulling back the red lever (16) mounted on the right-hand cockpit wall (*see* para. 34.)

(iii) The drop tank can be jettisoned by setting the DROP TANK JETTISONING switch to ON and pressing the release pushbutton. When the switch is ON a warning light next to the pushbutton comes on. This light goes out as the tank is released.

PART IV—EMERGENCIES

72. Parachute exits

(i) Whenever possible the pilot's and observer's entrance hatches should be used as parachute exits.
To open them pull the bottom catch release lanyards smartly, the airstream will then open the hatches and lock them.

> NOTE.—As the pilot's hatch opens the aircraft becomes tail heavy, but the change of trim is not great and can easily be held while retrimming.

(ii) After each minor inspection the operation of these hatches should be checked in flight at speeds between 130 and 220 knots (150 and 250 m.p.h.) I.A.S. For these tests the aircraft should be lightly loaded.

(iii) If the hatches open accidentally in flight it should be possible to close them again if

    (*a*) Pilot's hatch—the undercarriage is lowered;
                        the flaps are lowered 20°;
                        speed is reduced to 100 knots (115 m.p.h.) I.A.S.

    (*b*) Observer's hatch—speed is reduced below 175 knots (200 m.p.h.) I.A.S.

> WARNING.—With a torpedo slung these hatches cannot be used. If the torpedo cannot be jettisoned escape will have to be made through the crash exits (*see* para. 73).

73. Crash exits

In the event of a crash escape can be made

(i) through the roof of the pilot's cockpit;

(ii) through the right-hand window of the pilot's cockpit. The window is jettisoned by pulling back the release lever (53) on the lower frame and then pushing it outwards;

(iii) through the hood of the observer's cockpit. The release levers are on the port side of the fuselage.

PART IV—EMERGENCIES

74. Dinghies

A multi-seat dinghy is fitted in a blow-out stowage built into the trailing edge of the port wing. The dinghy is secured to the interior of the stowage structure by a light cord ; a pack containing rations, drinking water, paddles and recognition devices is stowed in the dinghy compartment and is connected to the dinghy by a lanyard. There are three alternative installations :

(i) A type " H " dinghy fitted with a type " G " operating head. With this installation provision is made only for manual release of the dinghy by the handle on the stowage cover.

(ii) A type " H " dinghy fitted with a type " H " operating head. In addition to an immersion switch for automatic operation of the type " H " head three manual releases are provided :

  (a) Internally, on the left-hand cockpit wall just behind the pilot's shoulder.

  (b) Internally, on the port side of the fuselage below the observer's hood.

  (c) Externally, forward of the leading edge of the fin.

(iii) A type " L " dinghy. This is operated as described in (ii) above.

In addition to the multi-seat dinghy there is provision for a " K " type dinghy both for the pilot and the observer.

75. Ditching (see A.P. 2095)

If ditching is unavoidable :

(i) Unlock the hoods of both cockpits, then swing the gunsight to the stowed position. If time permits the gunsight should be removed, by unscrewing the knurled nut half a turn, pulling out the electric supply plug and the quick release pin (which is on the right-hand side of the sight), and thrown into the well just behind the seat.

PART IV—EMERGENCIES

(ii) Keep the safety harnesses tightly adjusted. Disconnect the R/T plugs.

(iii) Keep the undercarriage retracted, but lower the flaps 30° to reduce the touch-down speed as much as possible.

(iv) Use the engines, if they are available, to ensure that the touchdown is made in a tail-down attitude at as low a forward speed as possible.

(v) Ditch along the swell or into wind if the swell is not steep.

> NOTE.—Deceleration is likely to be severe and much water may come over the nose and into the cockpit. As contact with the water is made a swerve is not unlikely.

A.P. 1721H—P.N.
Pilot's Notes

PART V
ILLUSTRATIONS

		Fig.
Cockpit—general view	... ...	1
Cockpit—port side	... ...	2
Cockpit—starboard side	... ...	3

KEY TO Fig. 1
COCKPIT GENERAL VIEW

1. Hydraulic power lever.
2. Hydraulic emergency selector lever.
3. Fuel contents gauges (port).
4. Undercarriage position indicators.
5. Radio altimeter.
6. Feathering pushbuttons.
7. R.P. selector switch.
8. Torpedo sight control.
9. Fire-extinguisher switches.
10. R.P. firing pushbutton.
11. Camera and gun firing switch.
12. Reflector gun sight.
13. Torpedo sight control switch.
14. Wheel brakes lever.
15. Torpedo and bomb selector switches.
16. R.P. rails jettison control lever.
17. Bomb fusing switches.
18. Rudder trim tab control.
19. Elevator trim tabs handwheel.
20. Windscreen de-icing pump.
21. Hydraulic handpump.
22. Elevator trim tab indicator.
23. Fuel pressure warning lights.
24. Electrical services switch.
25. Fuel jettison levers.
26. Undercarriage selector lever.
27. Flap control lever.

FIG. 1.

COCKPIT—GENERAL VIEW

KEY TO *Fig.* 2
COCKPIT—PORT SIDE

28. Destruction switches A.R.I. 5025.
29. Engine cut-out controls.
30. Fuel cock control levers.
31. Fuel crossfeed cock lever.
32. Drop tank fuel cock lever.
33. R.T. volume control.
34. Electric controller (radio).
35. Air intake controls.
36. Propeller speed controls.
37. Throttle controls.
38. Torpedo and bomb firing pushbutton.
39. Landing lamp switch.
40. Landing lamp control.
41. Supercharger controls.
42. Cowling gills controls and indicator lamps.
43. Drop tank pressure gauge.
44. Distress switch and master switch.

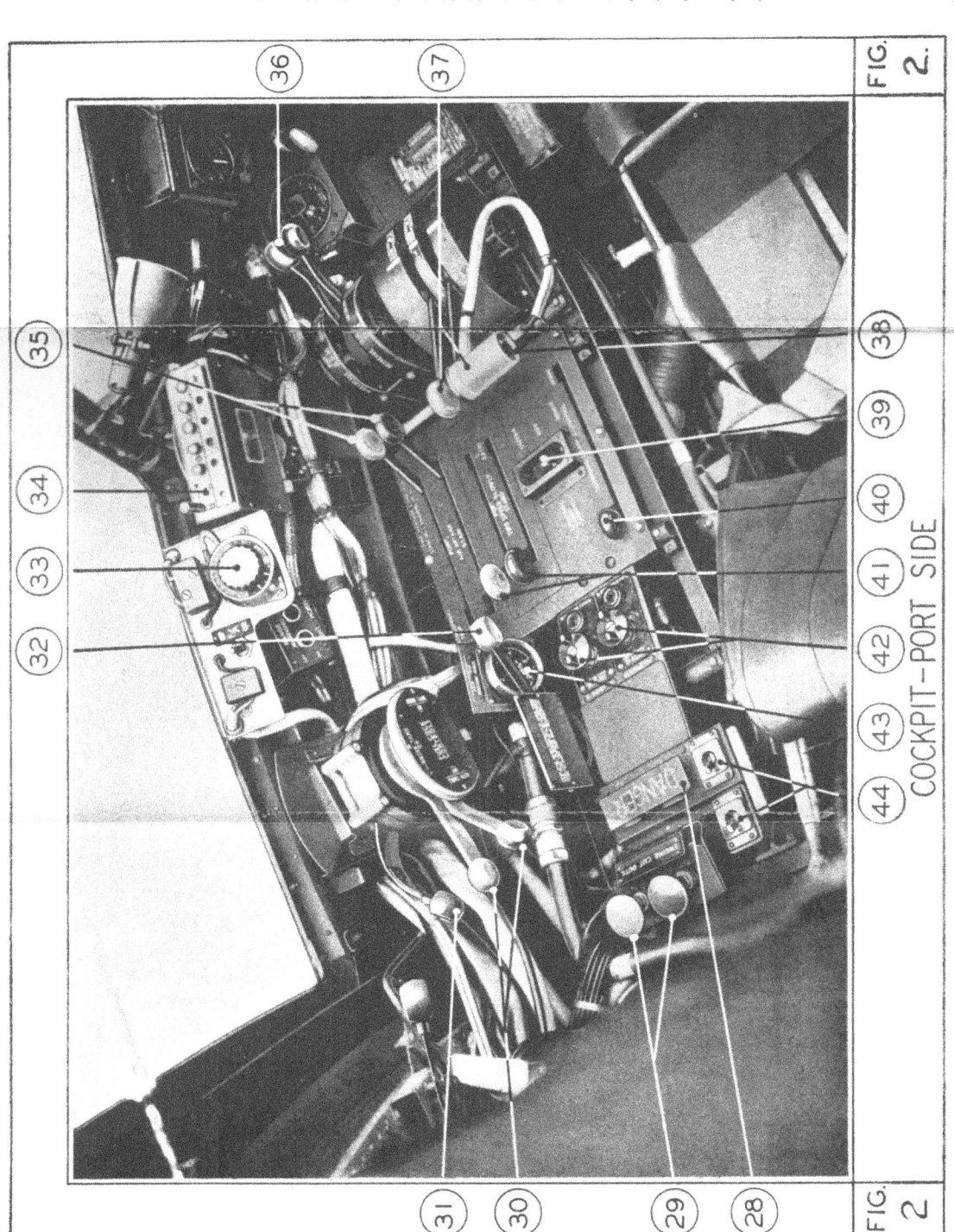

COCKPIT—PORT SIDE

FIG. 2

KEY TO *Fig.* 3
COCKPIT—
STARBOARD SIDE

45. Seat collapsing lever.
46. Bomb jettison switch.
47. Identification lights switch.
48. Navigation lights switch.
49. Pressure head heater switch.
50. Emergency light switch.
51. F46 camera switch.
52. R.I. compass switch.
53. Release handle—knock out panel.
54. Fuel contents gauges (starboard).
55. Fuel contents gauges (long range).
56. Aileron trim tab control.

ISBN #978-1-935327-74-5   1-935327-74-7

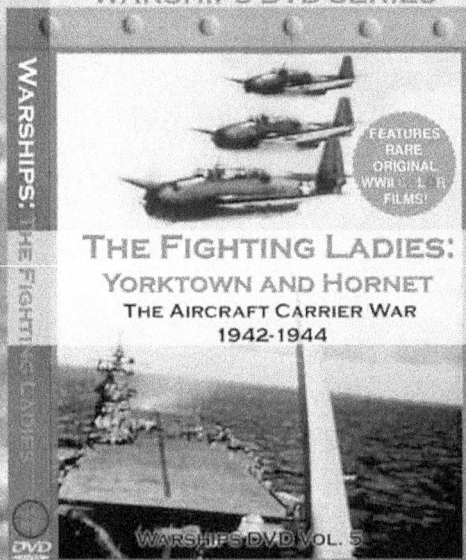

Aircraft At War DVD Series

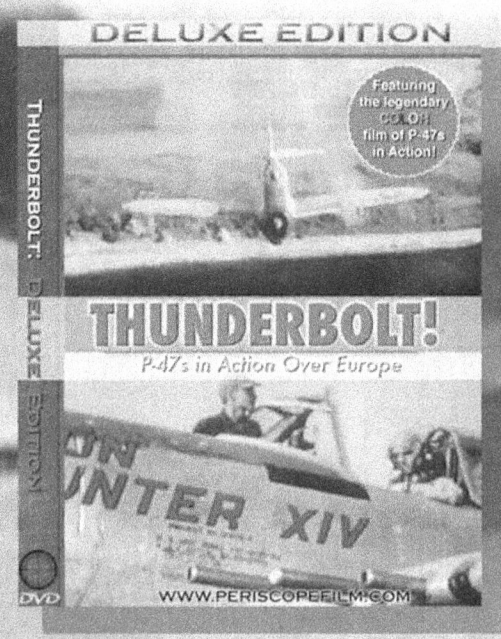
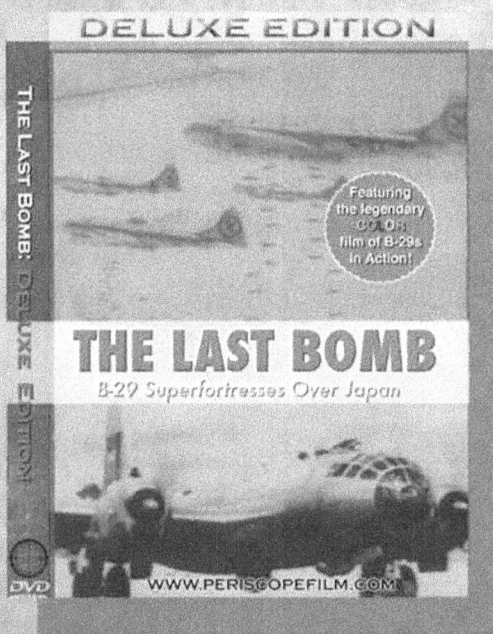
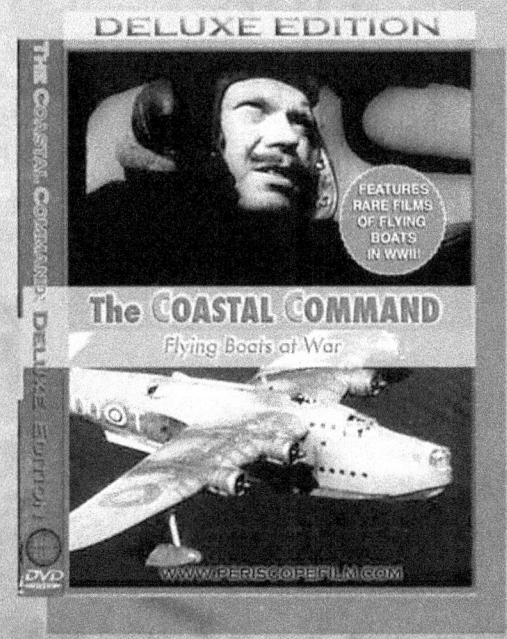

Now Available!

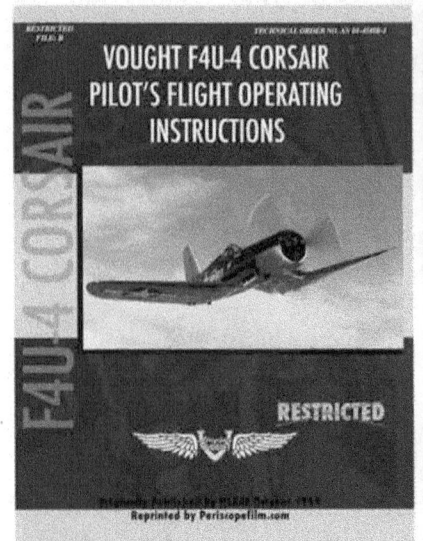
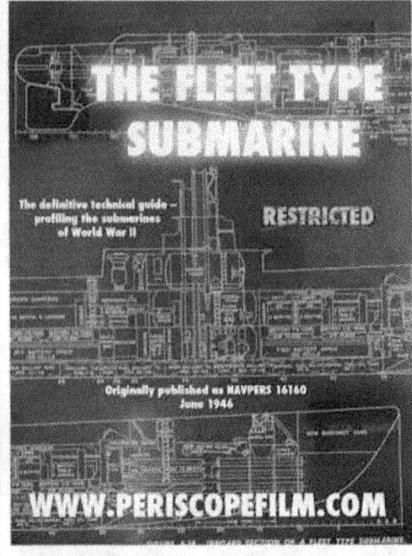

ALSO NOW AVAILABLE FROM PERISCOPEFILM.COM

www.ingramcontent.com/pod-product-compliance
Lightning Source LLC
Chambersburg PA
CBHW080521110426
42742CB00017B/3195